To Ted,
Good Hunting!
Mike Lapuli

2-28-97

HIGH PRESSURE ELK HUNTING

• SECRETS OF HUNTING EDUCATED ELK •

Mike Lapinski

HIGH PRESSURE ELK HUNTING

• SECRETS OF HUNTING EDUCATED ELK •

Mike Lapinski

Copyright 1996 by Mike Lapinski

ISBN 0-912299-63-0 (Hardcover)
ISBN 0-912299-64-9 (Softcover)

STONEYDALE PRESS PUBLISHING COMPANY
523 Main Street • Box 188
Stevensville, Montana 59870
Phone: 406-777-2729

Table of Contents

Prologue

The bull elk had only a few minutes to live when the enraged beast stomped up to an unfortunate lodgepole pine sapling and began ravaging the poor tree with his mighty rack of chocolate brown antlers. The poor young tree swayed and bent almost double as the bull grunted and pushed at it with his massive body.

The elk viciously raked the tree until the thin bark was peeled off it, leaving only a sappy white inner bark. With only a minute to live, the bull paused to sniff at the fragrant pungent aroma of pine sap.

Suddenly, a shrill bugle sounded from the other side of the lodgepole thicket and the bull's head snapped upward. His huge body trembled from a mixture of excitement and frustration. With less than 30 seconds to live, the bull slowly extended his head and emitted a low, furious bugle.

Before he had even finished bugling, his unseen adversary taunted him again. A low growl rumbled up from deep in the bull's chest. He spied a small opening in the thicket of trees and, with only a few seconds left in his life, the bull stomped forward to finally confront his tormentor.

The bull extended his neck and hissed a warning as he emerged from the thicket and stopped to eye the small opening ahead. He caught a slight movement to his left and was just turning to identify it when the arrow rammed deep into his chest.

I sank trembling to my knees and listened to the bull crash off. The wonderfully musty aroma of decaying forest debris and pine sap filled my nostrils and excited my senses. As I lay on the soft carpet of pine needles and luxuriated in the quiet solitude of the surrounding evergreen forest that rose toward the rugged mountain peaks in this wilderness paradise, I paused to say a little prayer of thankfulness to God for allowing me to once again experience this animal that I love so much. And then I prayed for a quick death.

Mike Lapinski
June 3, 1996

Introduction

Last September in Montana was hot and dry. It was literally short sleeve weather, even in the high country. I was in a backcountry elk camp with two other hunters, and you'd have thought the seventh plague had descended on us!

It was early in the rut and the bulls hadn't begun bugling heavily yet. I heard the same tired excuses: "It's too hot for the elk to rut! We need a frost to get them bugling!" I tried my best to make them understand that you could still successfully hunt silent bulls, but they decided to stick around camp and wait for the weather to cool off and get, "rutty."

I only hunted for two days. But in those two days, using the radical elk hunting method and an understanding of how to hunt silent bulls, I had four different rutting bulls within 20 yards. The first three got away, due to a swirling wind. The fourth didn't. On the evening of my second day hunting, I slipped in to within 80 yards of this fourth bull, who had grunted only once when I began bugling from a ridge 300 yards away.

My challenging bugle brought the five-point bull forward at a fast walk, and I shot him at 12 yards. The elk charged off, but piled up in a tangle of lodgepole blowdown after running just 100 yards.

The guys back at camp were flabbergasted! How? What? Why? I received an avalanche of questions that evening, and this time the guys were all ears to hear my radical philosophy on hunting rutting bull elk.

Something must have clicked afterwards, because I learned that one of the guys took a nice 5X5 bull, and the other passed up a

Public interest in elk and the mystique surrounding the difficulties of elk hunting has skyrocketed in recent years.

shot at 18 yards because he cared enough about the animal to avoid a risky shot through brush.

Since I wrote the *Radical Elk Hunting Strategies* book, I have received literally hundreds of letters and phone calls from fellow sportsmen who had finally achieved success taking rutting bull elk after reading my book. One fellow had never killed a bull after eight years of frustrated efforts, but he'd harvested two bulls in two years using the radical elk hunting method.

Still, things change. Nothing in this world stays the same. And in hunting, the most successful archer is one who is open to new understandings of the animal he pursues and improved hunting tactics. That's why this book is written.

Basically, it is an aid and an improvement to the radical elk hunting strategy. Make no mistake — the radical elk hunting strategy works and will always work. Yet even the successful hunters have come back with questions like, "Mike, have you ever seen the elk rut, but refuse to bugle? What should I do when that happens?"

These women and men are asking, "Is there more we can learn?" But more importantly they ask, "Is there more beyond the radical elk hunting philosophy to be learned?"

The answer is an emphatic YES! The *Radical Elk Hunting Strategies* book dealt with a specific issue. It was a very new and, well, radical departure from the accepted norm, and I believed I should stick with that subject entirely through the book.

But now, it's time to take up where the radical philosophy left off. Of course, even this book will be looked at as a radical approach because I don't intend to play it safe and give you readers milk toast. Yuck! You don't want fluff stuff with no substance.

Instead, you want meat! You want something substantial that has value. You want to know if the elk are really getting smarter. You want to know if the sudden surge of "new" elk calls, such as the mating and fighting cow calls, are fact or fantasy. And how about some "really radical" elk hunting methods? All these issues will be covered.

There is no doubt about it, elk hunting is changing. The high tech equipment is getting lighter and faster. Broadheads with spring loaded expanding blades are showing up in quivers. But are these innovations useful for elk hunting?

Even the hunting age group is changing. We're seeing more dedicated younger hunters who are aggressive, no-nonsense sportsmen. They've seen quite a few of their sporting heros caught in illegal, illicit, or unethical practices, and they seek some semblance of the old order of archers who didn't spend their time bragging themselves up.

Even the elk opportunities are changing. Habitat, or the lack of it in some areas, has greatly changed how the average bowhunter goes about pursuing the bull elk. New, but restrictive, trophy elk areas are popping up, but so is increased pressure.

Put all these changes together, and you can see the need for a more definitive book on the overall subject of elk hunting. The radical elk hunting philosophy will never change because it applies to the basic instincts of the rutting bull elk. However, even I have noticed a subtle change in the way bull elk respond as hunting pressure increases. So it is with great relish that we embark on paper to explore HIGH PRESSURE ELK HUNTING!

Chapter 1

Radical Elk Hunting Revisited

The radical elk hunting strategy was formulated and proven in the forests and mountains of Idaho and Montana. I successfully used it in a variety of terrain in Montana ranging from steep brush jungles along the Idaho border to open lodgepole and sage brush in central Montana.

So it was with some chagrin that immediately after the book appeared on the market, regional skeptics popped up saying, "It might work where you come from in Montana, but it won't work out here in Oregon." (or Arizona, or Colorado, etc. etc.)

Whereupon I went out to the thick brush of Oregon and killed a bull using the radical elk hunting method. So much for that skeptic. Then I went to Colorado and killed bulls in the oak brush jungles. So much for that argument. The radical elk hunting method also worked well in the open bull pine flats of New Mexico.

George Taulman of U.S. Outfitters, the largest outfitting business in the West, guides upwards to 500 elk hunters annually. One day George called to tell me that he fully agrees with the radical elk hunting philosophy. In fact, my book is required reading for all new guides he hires. His reason is simple. "It works," he told me.

Simply put, the radical elk hunting philosophy recognizes the rutting bull elk as an animal that goes through somewhat of a mating ritual. He tears up the brush and bugles out a challenge and warning to all other elk that he is the biggest and baddest elk in the woods.

With that done, he feels justified and is usually content to stomp off and sulk. Consequently, a bowhunter who hides behind a

This Colorado bull is further proof that the radical elk philosophy works in any region.

bush 200 yards away, hoping and praying the bull will come in and conveniently stand broadside at 20 yards, usually becomes frustrated and wonders if the problem is in his bugling or his camouflage, or a host of other doubts.

The one thing that the radical elk hunting philosophy has spawned is a brave new age of aggressive elk hunters. The radical elk hunter does not cringe behind some sapling praying that some distant rutting bull will have pity on him and come waltzing in to his calling like the Pied Piper.

Instead, the new elk hunter aggressively confronts the rutting bull. He moves in as close as possible before calling — forcing the bull to put up or shut up. And more often than not, he ends up with a dead bull at his feet.

Years ago, frustration also followed me on my elk hunts. The accepted elk hunting philosophy went something like this: If you could perfectly simulate a bull elk's bugle, any bull would come stomping in to your call. I got to be pretty good at bugling, but few bulls came all the way in. Instead, they seemed content to come in part way, rake their antlers and bugle up a storm, and then move off.

It was on a photo trip to Yellowstone National Park several years ago that I first got a glimpse of the rutting ritual of bull elk. One morning I observed several rutting elk bugling at each other from their own areas of a large meadow, but no confrontations or fights occurred. The bulls seemed content to bugle and be left alone.

It became obvious to me as I watched this wildlife spectacle that the accepted theory about good bugling bringing in bulls--simply was not true. Here were real bulls screaming at each other, yet no altercations occurred. There had to be something else that turned these bulls on.

As I was observing this phenomena, a wayward bull came over a low ridge and walked within 60 yards of a thicket where a resident bull was holed up. The wayward bull stopped to bugle, and that created an instant frenzied reaction from the resident bull. He immediately charged out of the thicket to confront the trespassing bull who would dare invade his area.

The resident bull raked his antlers in the grass and bugled up a storm until the trespassing bull moved off. That moment is really when the radical elk hunting strategy was born. I decided to simulate

The radical elk philosophy recognizes that bull elk go through somewhat of a mating ritual by bugling, raking trees, etc.

exactly what that trespassing bull had done — invade the security of another elk's domain.

I went back home to Idaho and it took only my first morning hunting to prove my theory. At first light a bull on a distant ridge answered my bugling. The bull shot back a reply to every one of my bugles, but it became obvious after a half hour that he was content to stay put. I slipped in close to the bull and was aided in locating him by his occasional bugling.

When I was within 70 yards, I dared not get closer or I ran the risk of him seeing me. I bugled and he immediately erupted with a furious bugle and began thrashing the brush with his antlers. I took that opportunity to slip in another 40 yards to an alder thicket.

I bugled again and that was just too much for the bull. He stomped forward to rout the brazen imp who had dared invade his domain with bugling insults. He came forward and began raking his antlers again. I took that opportunity to slip forward again to a spot that afforded good shooting lanes. Then I bugled.

The bull came looking for his adversary, and I shot him at 10 yards. He ran only 40 yards before dropping. That was my first

The radical elk hunter aggressively confronts a rutting bull in his own back door, forcing him to put up or shut up.

radical elk kill, and there have been many more since then in every conceivable type of terrain and cover.

Radical elk hunting relies on confrontation as its main tool. Think about it. Isn't that what any bull is doing when he bugles? He is confronting an adversary, real or imagined, to stay away from him. However, a long range confrontation usually does not end up with a dead elk. Most bulls simply won't leave their home area and cross mountains and streams just to get a look at their challenger.

But move in close, literally at his back door, and there are very few bulls who will not come forward out of anger, frustration, or curiosity to see what their challenger looks like.

Even when I encounter that one bull in 20 who will come hundreds of yards to my bugling, I like to move forward. Actually, that's one of the secrets to my high success rate. I've learned that if I hide behind a bush and wait for the bull to come into range, he gets to pick the ambush spot. He may come in on the downwind side, or through an area that is choked with brush where a shot is impossible.

While the bull is coming in, I'll move forward and pick a spot that will put me on the downwind side with good shooting lanes. As

A rutting bull usually reacts angrily to a sudden bugle just out of his sight and will stomp forward either from curiosity or to confront his adversary.

a result, I kill about half the bulls that come forward.

Radical elk hunting not only calls for quick movement, it also requires quick shooting. Don't expect a long drawn out encounter. Often times, I'm releasing an arrow within a few minutes of when I confront a bull in his domain. At the sound of my sudden challenge so close to his lair, a bull usually starts immediately in my direction.

Consequently, when I set up to make a radical challenge, I make sure my ambush spot is perfect, the wind is in my favor, and an arrow is nocked. Last fall, I slipped in to about 100 yards of a five-point bull in open timber. I was using a grunt tube with a string that kept the bugle slung back over my shoulder when not in use.

I bugled, and to my amazement, the bull was headed in my direction at a brisk pace. I barely had time to get the grunt tube slung back over my shoulder before the bull was within range. I shot the bull at 12 yards, and the elk fell dead within a hundred yards. I didn't have a stop watch to time the event, but I'd guess that the entire confrontation took less than a minute from bugle to kill. That's fast!

One of the keys to success for the radical elk hunter is to understand what kind of bull elk is out there in front of him. I have identified three different "emotional subspecies" of rutting bull elk, and all three often require different hunting tactics.

First, there is the immature bull who has not yet reached maturity. He'll come in bugling, but then break off contact at the last second and drift away. He is unsure of himself, especially after getting roughed up a few times by the bigger bulls.

It's easy to identify an immature bull by the squeaky sound of his bugle and his smallish ragged set of antlers. Hence the name "raghorn," which means small bull. These are very easy bulls to kill early in the season before they get horned a few times, but I've also had success with raghorns later in the rut by toning down my calling and making myself sound like just another young bull who wants to have fun.

Second is the frustrated bachelor bull who is physically mature, but unable to mate because the bigger herd bull has jealously herded them into a harem and will not share. Obviously, this is the easiest bull to call in with either bugling or cow calls.

The best way to identify a bachelor bull is by the deep, mature sound of his bugle and the absence of cows in the area. Actually, it's easy to tell if the bull is alone because a half dozen cows milling around 80 yards away make an awful lot of commotion, and they are constantly mewing back and forth.

Cow calls are especially good when a bachelor bull is encountered, but a challenging bugle also works well because a bachelor bull is often consumed by lust and frustration. I swear, sometimes just about any sound from a cow call to a car horn is enough to bring one of these rangy bachelor bulls on the run.

The herd bull is the most impressive animal among the hierarchy of bull elk. He is also the most difficult to successfully hunt. If the bull in front of you immediately returns your bugle, but is farther away the next time he bugles, he's probably a herd bull and he's moving his cows away from the competition. You'll also hear lots of brush snapping and hooves pounding as the cows move through the forest, emitting their bird-like chirps as they go.

I've had success with the herd bull by charging forward and

The best method for success is to move forward quickly and confront a rutting bull before he has a chance to perform his "Tough Guy" rutting ritual and then slip away.

getting as absolutely close to the cows as possible before bugling. A retreating herd bull will sometimes turn back to rout the brazen bull who would dare slip in so close to his cows.

Hunting the herd bull is a long shot, at best. However, success is possible. I've been able to kill three herd bulls after I bugled from a position near the cows. They were my most difficult hunts, but they also represent my most impressive trophy racks.

That is radical elk hunting in its abridged form as an appetizer to whet your appetite for things to come. If you have not yet read the book *Radical Elk Hunting Strategies*, I would suggest you get a copy of it because there is a wealth of biological and hunting information that will greatly aid you in your quest to understand the elk. (See Appendix B, page 191, for address.)

But as I mentioned, I would be a self-centered fool to say that *Radical Elk Hunting Strategies* is the absolute last word on the subject of early season elk hunting. Nothing stays the same, especially in our age of changing habitat and increasing pressure. So it is with great relish that we attack the first and most important question concerning high pressure elk hunting. Are the bulls getting smarter?

Back in 1970, a toot on a crude flute-like pipe bugle would cause an immediate reaction from a rutting bull elk.

Chapter 2

Are Bull Elk Getting Smarter?

An older fellow I know told me that he couldn't understand why I was writing a book about bugling elk. He said, "Back in 1959 when I worked as a packer, I could get a response from any bull elk by whistling into an empty rifle casing."

That same man recalled a particular incident with a rutting bull when he was working as a packer back in the early 1960's. He was packing supplies into a Forest Service camp in North Idaho in the middle of September, and every time he brought his pack string of mules across a low saddle, a rut crazed bull would came charging out of the nearby timber and shake his antlers at the bewildered mules.

His yelling and swearing just seemed to fire the bull up even more. After the third time over that saddle, the stock almost stampeded when the bull made several false charges. The next time through, my old packer friend brought along his .30-06. Sure enough, when the bull heard the mules' hooves clomping nearby, he bugled furiously and broke cover in a fast trot. The packer ended that rut crazed bull's short reign of terror with one well placed bullet.

Things have sure changed since then, haven't they? Today, sportsmen struggle to understand changing behavior patterns in bull elk over the past several years. Elk that once came right in, now circle downwind and slip in silently. In some areas they have almost quit bugling, and hunters are at a loss to explain this phenomenon except to conclude that the bulls are just getting smarter than they used to be.

I've spent 30 years observing elk in the wild, and I've been a student of elk behavior. I've watched a host of various environmental and social changes create a condition that has forced the elk to react. Yes, I too have noticed the change.

But are bull elk getting smarter? The answer is an emphatic NO! Bull elk are not getting smarter, in an academic sense. Elk are animals and lack the capability to gain knowledge and intelligence. Elk, like all animals, tend to simply react instinctively to their environment.

And therein lies the real question of the "Smart Elk" issue. Basically, the question should be rephrased to read something like this: Are bull elk reacting differently as their environment changes? The answer to that question is YES!

Please do not write off my subtle play on words as cute prose. How we look at this change in elk behavior has a great effect on how we will hunt today's elk. If elk are truly getting smarter, we're in big trouble! Coupled with its superior natural instincts and this newly found intelligence, elk could literally outthink us. They'd take a look at the calendar, note when hunting season opened, and make sure they were in the safety of a wildlife refuge or private property where hunting was not allowed!

Fortunately, that is not true, and it is the hunter who understands why elk have changed who will be able to identify why it behaves differently and then adapt his hunting techniques. I have, and my success with these "Smart Elk" has not dropped off.

When I first began hunting bull elk back in 1970 in Idaho, we used a piece of plastic pipe with a notch cut out and a slotted plug inserted. This curious call created a variety of noises ranging from a decent high pitched whistle to a hollow whine.

Often times, you had no idea what sound would come from your bugle due to the swelling of the wooden plug or its shifting inside the tube. More than once, I blew nothing but a gush of air out the end of my bugle because the plug had fallen out!

No matter, the bulls reacted with frenzied excitement to these crude bugles, and we killed them. But after a few years of hunting in a drainage, the bulls were not as quick to come charging forward at the sound of our crude flutes.

At about the same time, three Arkansas hunters went on their first elk hunt to Colorado and discovered that their turkey calling mouth diaphragms could be made to sound exactly like a bull elk's

Are elk getting smarter? The answer is no, but they are adapting very well to changing conditions.

bugle. Sorry folks. I know there are a lot of elk experts who have claimed this invention, but I remember reading the article by these Arkansas men in an archery magazine in 1974. With the latex turkey diaphragm blown into a hollow tube, the hollow high pitched sound it made almost perfectly simulated the bugle of a rutting bull elk.

For years, we who had adapted by using a turkey mouth call and vacuum cleaner hose, were able to achieve remarkable success. But eventually, everyone in the woods began blowing on new and improved commercial elk bugles, and the elk were not as quick to come charging in to a challenging call, no matter how authentic it sounded.

It's gotten to the point today where the only way you can bring a bull elk in to your calling is to convince him that you truly are another elk at the end of the sound.

How did it get this way? How did we lose the edge we once enjoyed over the rutting bull elk? In my opinion the answers lie in two areas: changing environment and increased hunting pressure.

For several years, we early elk bowhunters who used a turkey diaphragm and vacuum cleaner hose achieved remarkable success.

We all know about the elk's eventual disappearance from its historic home range on the Great Plains as settlers took over those fertile lands for farms. However, the elk adapted quite well to life in mountainous and forested terrain. The elk set up a life cycle that was comfortable and the species proliferated. Eventually, human civilization began to encroach on this secluded elk habitat until the elk could no longer continue their normal cycle of nature, so they were forced to adapt again, and then again and again.

This changed the basic nature of the animal we call the elk into a reclusive backcountry dweller. In other words, the elk adapted. However, we pioneers of elk archery hunting who slipped into these backcountry lairs of the bull elk 30 years ago found prime hunting for rutting bulls.

I remember that elk archery kills were so rare back in the 1970's that I used to get my picture on the front page of the paper when I brought back a bow-killed bull elk from the backcountry.

As more roads pushed back into the wilderness areas, more hunters came and the elk adapted. Yes, elk still prefer to live far back from civilization. However, we're now seeing some elk that actually prefer to live closer to roads and alfalfa fields. They seek out impenetrable thickets during the day and move into the croplands at dusk. They too have adapted well to their changing environment.

I believe that increased hunting pressure, often reaching the intolerable level, has also had a great impact on the way elk react today. At one time, a mature bull elk that weighed upward to a half ton didn't have to fear any predator, be it mountain lion or wolf.

But even the biggest bulls went down in a heap from a well placed .30-06 bullet, or a razor sharp arrow. It was only the bulls who instinctively reacted when threatened, that lived to rut another day. But eventually, most of the bigger bulls fell prey to hunters.

In my area of western Montana, this is especially true. Back in 1978 when I first began hunting along the Idaho border, it was not unusual to see a half dozen herd bulls during the rut that would score above 300 points.

My favorite hunting area was only a mile back in from a four lane freeway, but most hunters just didn't want to work that hard to kill an elk, so I had the area all to myself. But through the years,

Forest Service roads have encroached into this area. Now, hunters can drive right into the heart of what was once prime backcountry elk hunting country.

I have watched with sadness as the quality of the bull elk in this area slowly dwindled. Today, it is not unusual to go through the entire archery season and not see a bull over 300 points. In fact, it's not unusual to see a small four-point bull who is only 2 1/2 years old proudly leading a harem of cows. This is typical of many of the areas that have become over-roaded and over-hunted, especially on public land.

This sudden removal of the older mature bull elk from the hierarchy of the elk herd has caused the entire rutting ritual to change. It's little wonder that the bulls don't bugle like they used to. The pecking order of older mature bachelor bull, frustrated mature bachelor bull and foolish immature bull is simply not there in many areas where hunting pressure is heavy.

Take Oregon, for example. There are only three mature bulls per hundred cows in that state. You can't expect to blow on your cow call and have a bull come charging forward. He's got a hundred cows out there to choose from!

In some areas of Arizona where hunting pressure is very heavy, the bulls seldom come in to the bugling challenge of a hunter. And in Colorado where heavy hunting pressure and a four-point or better law exists, there are literally hundreds of 2 1/2 year old four-point bulls running around in confusion during the rut. They don't know whether they're raghorns, bachelor bulls, or herd bulls!

That's the bad news. The good news is that there are still areas where quality bull elk exist today — even on public land. And it is still possible to successfully call in these bulls, no matter what their size is. However, just as the elk have been forced to adapt, we hunters must also adapt our hunting styles to counter the change in the rutting patterns of the elk.

That's not to say that the elk of today are a subspecies of yesterday's elk. We must remember that the elk remain the same species, with the same instincts no matter what pressure is present. We can liken today's high pressure elk to a pack of wolves I recently observed in a pen.

When wolves are put into captivity, a curious phenomenon

Hunting pressure in many areas has forced the bigger bulls to either adapt to changing conditions or be killed.

occurs. Even though these wilderness dwellers are taken from their natural environment and thrown into a totally foreign habitat and lifestyle, they maintain their identity as wolves.

I watched in amazement as 13 wolves in a four acre enclosure set up their family pack hierarchy exactly as it would have been in the backcountry. The alpha male dominated the pack, and the alpha female was his second in command. The only mating allowed was by the alpha male and female, and discipline was meted out severely to any wolf who strayed from the pack's identity.

This is also true of the elk, no matter what environment they live in or how much pressure they endure. They are still elk. The cows communicate by mewing at each other, and the bulls still rut every fall and compete for the right to mate the cows.

Remember my favorite hunting area in western Montana where the hunting had increased so much? Well, it seems that the elk still proliferated to the point that they began damaging crops. A special January depredation rifle hunt was done, and 25 cow elk were harvested. Each hunter had a warden at his side when he killed his

The good news is that elk are still basically the same animal, even under pressure. They rut, fight and mate, but they have changed somewhat in their reaction to a bugling challenge.

cow, and pregnancy tests were made.

Of the 25 cows tested, 23 were pregnant, with the dates of conception all falling within the time frame of September 15-21. You see, even when hunting pressure is heavy, the elk still rut and they still mate.

Therein lies the real secret of success for hunting today's "high pressure" elk. Simply put, the elk have adapted, so we must adapt. It's not that hard, either. My Radical Elk Hunting Philosophy, if you will remember, identified the bull elk as a creature of habit who performed a mating ritual, and the key to success for the radical elk hunter was to move in and confront that rutting elk — no matter whether he was bugling up a storm or just raking his antlers on the brush.

Yes, the elk have changed, but that doesn't mean that the overall elk hunting experience has been diluted. On the contrary! We archers relish the challenge of the hunt more than the killing. That's why we've limited ourselves to hunting with the bow and arrow. And there certainly is a wonderful challenge out there. I've discovered that an encounter with a rut crazed bull elk today is just as exciting as it was back in 1970 when I killed my first bull.

They may not bugle as much, but when you have one of those huge brutes punishing a tree not more than 15 yards away, the thrill is just as intense, and the satisfaction just as complete when you put that arrow exactly where it's supposed to go for a humane kill.

Let's take the next step toward success in hunting the high pressure bull elk by looking at the new elk calls. There are several new game calls on the market today that claim to be just the thing for luring in high pressure bulls. And from all the hype surrounding them, it's sure to confuse the average bowhunter.

Though elk have adapted to a changing environment and increased hunting pressure, they are still elk and the thrill of a close range encounter is still there.

Chapter 3

The New Elk Calls

As I mentioned, the diaphragm elk bugle and cow call revolutionized elk calling and allowed many sportsmen to fool elk — for a while. But as we are all painfully aware, overcalling, stupid calling, and too many callers have created a condition where the elk simply are not fooled just because you can bugle like a real bull.

Other than a few improvements by call manufacturers to make their calls easier to use, there have been no "new" calls appear commercially for the past several years. However, that's all changed. Several new elk calls have hit the market. These new calls produce sounds that are different from the standard elk bugle and cow call that have been the elk hunting standard. Unfortunately, there have been subtle claims by some of the manufacturers that their calls will bring in any bull in the area because of this newly discovered elk sound.

You can imagine how some of these new calls appealed to the average frustrated elk hunter. For only $5.95, the luckless archer could purchase a revolutionary new elk call that would prove irresistible to a bull elk. With great interest I investigated these new calls to learn exactly what "new" sounds were being marketed. Of course, in the back of my mind was the thought, "Boy, if they work, I want one!"

I have always been intrigued by the complex social structure of the elk, and I've spent an average of two weeks each fall just observing and photographing rutting elk all over the West. I've become intimately knowledgeable of the very private world of the elk. In my opinion, that's the main reason why I've been successful

Bull elk do not have some sort of secret language that only they understand. They simply react to their environment.

harvesting elk — because I understand them. Elk sounds especially interest me because both bull and cow elk emit a variety of sounds, and these sounds mean different things to the elk.

Let's take a moment to examine some of the facts and fallacies of elk sounds, and we'll begin with the elk bugle. The elk bugle is nothing more than a bull elk vocalizing his presence during the rut. To an elk, there is no difference between the classic three note bugle, or a euck, or any combination thereof.

I recently read a book that stated that bull elk mean certain things by the sounds of their bugle. The author justified this thinking by noting that he'd once watched a bull amiably feeding while three other bulls bugled around him, but the feeding bull bugled only after one of the bulls had called. He concluded that the one bull in particular was saying something in elk talk that disturbed the feeding bull. To me, that sounds like a lot of bull!

If he'd observed closer, he'd have realized that the bull was simply bugling about once every five minutes like most rutting elk do. He was not responding to a specific "secret elk language" taunt.

These are the types of misconceptions that wreak havoc on elk hunters! They read this stuff and become very confused when their "elk bugling language" isn't compatible with the elk talk. And of course they continue buying any new calls that claim to offer that "secret" sound.

Let me categorically state, after several thousand hours of intently studying rutting bull elk: The is no secret bull elk language! Elk are simply animals who react to their environment!

Cow elk are a different matter. Certain sounds emitted by a cow are specific in meaning. The soft, bird-like chirp of a cow elk is a social form of communication. When a cow calls she's saying, "Here am I; where are you?" It is the very basic herding sound that keeps cow elk in touch with each other.

However, an alert cow will raise the pitch of her call, and it will sound more shrill and tense. Every elk within hearing will immediately stop what they are doing to study the area for danger. If danger is identified, in the form of a lion, bear or man, a cow will emit a coarse bark, and the entire herd will become alert and

Elk have a very complex social structure, and they call back and forth to each other all year.

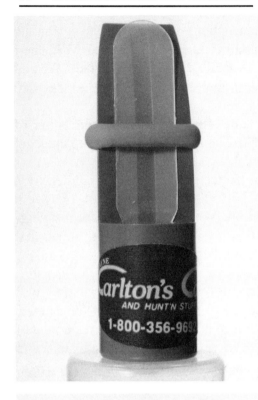

The Wayne Carlton Fighting Cow Call is a legitimate "new sound" elk call that may trigger a bull's interest when the rut is on.

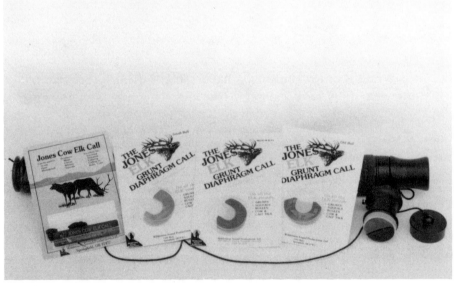

Some of the new elk bugles on the market represent a honing and refining of existing calls, such as these Jones calls. Larry D. Jones expects to have a new elk call on the market soon.

prepare to flee.

These are the basic bull and cow calls that have for so many years been the basis for calling in elk. They were biologically sound and universally accepted. So when new calls came out recently that proposed "new" sounds that were made by elk, they caused a stampede to sporting goods stores by paranoid, frustrated elk archers who were convinced by their failure that it was their calling that had failed them. (In reality, it was their lack of understanding of elk that was at the root of their problems.)

New Bull Elk Calls

Surprisingly, most of the new elk bugles fresh on the market are of the good kind. They represent a honing and refining of manufactured calls to sound more like a bull elk's bugle. This is good news because, frankly, the majority of the commercial elk bugles sounded dreadful unless used by a pro.

However, avoid those few that guarantee they'll produce a sound that will bring any bull in on the run because their tone will produce that magic sound that enrages a bull elk. This stuff is hype. However, even such false claims laid on these bugles do not disqualify them as useful tools to confront and force a bull to put up or shut up.

New Cow Calls

While the new bull calls have remained fairly conventional, the new cow calls have caused a tremendous commotion among the elk hunting public. Some of these calls claim that new, previously unheard sounds, are being made by elk. And by simulating these new sounds, astronomical success is possible. Let's take a look at these new calls.

Mating Cow Call

This call supposedly is an urgent, shrill sound that a cow in heat uses to let the bull know she is getting in the mood to mate. The sound of this call is supposed to simulate a female impatient to get on with the mating process. The theory is that any bull elk will come looking for the cow that emits this call and then stay close by until she is ready to mate.

I have watched 13 matings in the wild, and been around countless herd bulls with cows, and I have never heard this high pitched, pleading call. Of course, this is just my observation, but surely, if such a sound was emitted by a cow elk when she wanted a bull to stay close, I believe I would have heard it.

Fighting Cow Call

The concept of the fighting cow call is that cows in competition will emit a long-drawn-out call that almost sounds like a squeaky spike bull call. The theory is that any elk hearing this call of agitation and confrontation will come forward to investigate. There is also the idea here that the cow is impatiently awaiting the attention of a rutting bull.

Last fall in Yellowstone National Park, I located a herd of about 12 cows with a large herd bull. For some reason, the cows became very frisky and began emitting a cow call that was drawn out and filled with excitement. The entire herd of cows became charged with excitement and soon the entire herd was squealing this drawn out cow call. It was very enjoyable to observe this high state of excitement and activity among the cows.

Unfortunately, the herd bull did not share my enthusiasm. He continued to feed through this raucous deluge of aggressive (fighting) cow calls. However, I want to state that this call does exist in the elk herd. It is a variation of the standard cow call. It is more urgent and drawn out and often precludes a confrontation between cows.

Also, I've seen a herd of cows become very agitated and vocal when one or more begin to go into heat, and a cow in heat often becomes very irritable and strikes out at any cows that approach her. Consequently, the agitated/fighting cow call is a legitimate elk sound that may trigger a bull's interest when the rut is on.

Receptive Cow Call

The theory behind this call is that when a cow is ready to mate, she emits a low whining sound that tells any nearby bull that she is ready to receive him. As I mentioned, I have watched 13 matings of elk in the wild, sometimes as close as 20 yards away — and I have never heard this sound. I have also pored through

A rutting bull elk pays special attention to a cow when she is about to go into heat.

respected elk biology books stuffed with scientific data, but I have found no mention of such a sound being made by a cow who is ready to be mated.

My observations of elk matings were virtually identical. The bull would regularly inspect his harem of cows by sniffing at their rear ends. For no apparent physical reason, he would single out a particular female, even though no sounds were emitted. The bull would nuzzle the cow, and often times the cow would nuzzle back, or show extreme submission to the bull.

I learned from academic books that a cow elk that was going into heat began passing a female hormone in her urine and out her vagina, which acted as an attractant to the bull that the cow was nearing her receptive stage. These female hormones then triggered the release of pheromones, an odiferous substance that caused a sexual response in both the female and male elk. The cow would then stand in front of the bull and arch her rear end, often spreading her legs to better receive the bull.

The bull would nuzzle and lick the cow's vagina and become fully excited and erect. The bull would then raise up on his hind legs and ejaculate into the cow with one violent thrust. During every one of these matings, I never heard an elk sound uttered.

From these observations I've just passed on, you may conclude that all the new cow calls are counterfeit. Not quite! I've used Wayne Carlton's Fighting Cow Call to add excitement to my calling, and the elk generally responded to this mixing up of the calls. More than once, I've had bulls turning away with disinterest at my standard cow calling, but when I emitted a few fighting cow calls, the bull responded with curiosity and came forward. This is a good call to add to your calling arsenal.

The Secret of Successful Elk Calling

The critical requirement of successful calling is to make the elk think you are a real elk doing the calling. But to become truly successful you must put some excitement into your calling.

My friend, Larry D. Jones, told me that on one balmy afternoon in Oregon last fall, he'd hiked into an area and met two bowhunters who told him the area was dead. The men claimed the elk were either not there or were not rutting. Larry had hunted the

Some elk call developers with plenty of field experience, like Dale Burk of Snowcrest Outdoor Products, have designed calls to cover a wide range of elk sounds, from the softer mew of a cow through the immature, squeaky sound of a raghorn bull on to the deeper, mature grunts and melodic bugle of a satellite or herd bull.

area before, and he knew the bulls usually rutted in that area, so he hiked down the trail and began bugling and cow calling. His calling increased in frequency and urgency until a bull finally answered him.

Larry then moved forward and began aggressive cow calling and bugling until that entire drainage lit up with bugling elk. Larry used no new elk sound. There was no Pied Piper effect. Instead, he created an excitement in his calling that aroused the elk and caused them to respond.

A few years ago in north Idaho I met three thoroughly defeated bowhunters as I hiked into an area that looked like prime elk habitat. They were leaving the area after getting very little response to their calling, and they warned me that I was wasting my time.

I hiked up to a ridge top that afforded a good view of the upper end of the drainage where the elk should be congregated. I began bugling. Not once every 15 minutes, but constantly. I made long, drawn-out bugles, short grunts, cow calls. You name it, I made it, over and over again. Within a half hour, I had bulls bugling and cows calling everywhere.

A bull bugled from a low ridge about 300 yards upstream from me. The wind was right, so I moved in as the bull continued to bugle, which conveniently allowed me to keep his location pinpointed. I eased forward cautiously when I approached the area where his calling had come from. I finally heard the unmistakable dull grating sound of the bull raking his antlers on a tree. I took that opportunity to ease forward until I was only about 60 yards from the bull.

I studied the area and decided that the bull would come through an opening in the dense brush on my left. I nocked an arrow, sucked in a deep breath, and bugled. Then I scooted forward about 15 yards to a spot where a large bush grew about 15 yards from the opening.

I had just dropped to one knee and brought my bow up when the bull bugled. Heavy hoof beats sounded on the forest floor and I could hear the sound of antlers swishing through the brush. A moment later, the five-point bull pushed through the thicket and into the opening.

I picked a tuft of hair about six inches behind his shoulder, drew back, and released. The arrow buried nock deep in the bull's chest, and he stumbled as he turned to run. A half hour later, I was admiring a beautiful trophy bull. If I'd listened to those other bowhunters, I would have missed one of my most enjoyable elk hunts.

Wayne Carlton is another expert elk hunter who agrees with the idea of putting excitement in his calling. Wayne told me, "I start out with the standard cow and bull cows, but I'll go to the fighting cow call if that doesn't work. Then I'll go to a bugle, then a cow call. I will use any and every elk sound. Whatever it takes to get the elk excited."

There is sound biological reason behind the tactic of working the rutting elk herd into a frenzy of excitement through aggressive calling. Though bull elk may bugle for three weeks or more during the rut, the cow elk come in heat for a relatively short time. The normal activity of a herd bull during the rut is to bugle and chase other bulls away from his cows.

Aggressive calling when the elk are quiet will often get you a shot when other elk hunters have given up.

As he moves through his harem, he is constantly sniffing at the cows for any sign of a discharge of pheromones, which would signal the female is in heat and ready for mating. The average cow elk comes into heat for a very short period of about 18 hours. During this time, the bull will mount her several times.

He is worked up into a frenzy of bugling and rutting activity as the pheromones push his mating urge to an intense level. Other bulls in the area catch the scent of the cow in heat, or notice the increased emotion in the elk herd, and also open up with impassioned bugling. The cows become very jumpy and edgy as the rampaging herd bull roughly inspects them.

I have observed this scenario many times. We call it the peak of the rut, and it is a wildly exciting time in the elk woods. The cows are milling and calling back and forth; they're fighting and chasing each other, the herd bull is in constant motion mating one or more cows and then chasing other bulls away.

The sounds and action of this peak rut period are exactly what

Larry D. Jones does not let warm temperatures discourage him. This big Arizona bull is proof that Larry can put lots of excitement into his calling at any time of day in any type of weather.

an experienced hunter is trying to accomplish when he says he is trying to put some excitement into his calling. He is literally simulating the frenzied action and various elk calls associated with the peak rut period.

You can also see how an inexperienced elk hunter could become confused by the lethargy in an elk herd during the rut. Many times I've had hunters tell me a particular drainage was dead. They'd had only a few responses to their bugling, and none of the bulls seemed interested in coming in. In reality, those bulls were in rut and ready to mate any cow in heat. They were just waiting for the peak rut period when the cows were receptive.

I'd go in after them and begin bugling and cow calling. Not the standard "once every 15 minutes" stuff either. I'd bellow out enormous bugles, sometimes three or four per minute for several minutes. I'd emit impassioned cow calls — soft mews and long-drawn-out fighting cow calls. The bulls in the area became worked up into a frenzy because they identified this sudden increase in activity as peak rut when one or more cows were in heat.

I've killed many rut crazed bull elk early in the rut, during hot weather, at midday, when the other hunters had given up bowhunting for a few days until the weather cooled off and the elk began to rut. Ha!

Larry D. Jones told me, "I killed a nice bull last year in Oregon at three in the afternoon when the temperature was almost 90 degrees. If you can put enough excitement in your calling to make a bull believe the cows are in heat, that bull's gonna come looking no matter what time of day or temperature it is."

In closing, some of the new elk calls are biologically sound, and some are really stretching it. Don't fall into the trap of thinking that some new call is going to emit a sound that will bring in every bull.

Instead, put some excitement into your calling. When you bugle, think of how a rut crazed bull elk would feel, and then put some feeling into that bugle. Do the same thing with the cow calls. Draw out that soft mew to make the cow sound aggressive and fighting mad because she is in heat and other cows are bothering her. You'll be amazed at how much more responsive the elk become to your calling.

The critical elk encounter is that wonderfully tense confrontation when hunter and bull elk first make contact.

Chapter 4

The Critical Elk Encounter

There is a time during the elk hunt that is so charged with drama that just the mention of it shoots a rush of adrenalin through an experienced elk hunter's veins. True, being in the woods during the rut and hearing the elk bugling is awfully exciting, but there comes a point during the hunt when all the preliminaries are over with, and it's time for action.

It's called the critical elk encounter — that very special, wonderfully tense confrontation when hunter and rut crazed bull elk first make contact. It is during this initial, bittersweet meeting of elk and man when success, or failure, is determined, depending upon how it is handled by the hunter.

Soldiers will tell you that it is during that initial contact with the enemy that victory or defeat in battle is decided. It's no different with elk hunting. If I can encounter that incoming bull on my terms, I can usually kill him. This may surprise you, but I can usually tell within the first minute of that initial contact with a bull whether or not the hunt will be a success.

There seems to be a certain surreal tempo at which my successful elk encounters have unfolded. I'm not alone. Other experienced elk hunters tell me that they too can sense when things are right, and they too have noticed this awesome drama unfolding at a rapid, almost predestined, pace.

That's why I have identified the initial encounter with a rutting bull elk as the critical point in any hunt. Think about it. You've done your homework and succeeded in locating a rutting elk. Your calling has a bull excited. He is not only responding, but he is

The break in contact between hunter and rutting bull elk is the single most frustrating thing that the average elk hunter will encounter.

also coming forward. In fact he may be so close that you can see or hear him.

At this point, the bull may be almost within bow range. You've done everything right so far, and you only have to do one more thing to claim your trophy — you have to put an arrow into his chest. As simple as this last chore appears, most bowhunters fail to accomplish it.

Actually, it's not too difficult to get to that critical encounter stage with a bull elk, even for the person with limited elk savvy. During the rut the bulls are milling around looking for cows, they're vocal, and often times they're not too picky about the sound of a hunter's bugle.

But from that point on, things often fall apart for the average bowhunter because he has no plan for how he'll get that bull broadside at 20 yards. Consequently, the bull is prone to hang up. A hangup occurs when a bull is coming forward, but then hangs up out of range. He may continue bugling and raking his antlers, but eventually the bull will lose interest and move off.

This break in contact between the hunter and what appeared

The obvious solution to the hangup problem is to shoot an oncoming bull as he approaches the area where the calling came from.

to be a promising encounter with a rut crazed bull elk is the single most frustrating thing that the average bowhunter encounters. I receive hundreds of phone calls and letters from sportsmen every year, and the topic of hangups is always at the top of their list of questions. I can see how a bewildered bowhunter might accuse his traitorous bugle of being demon possessed and secretly emitting a silent warning to an oncoming bull elk.

The key to solving the problem of a hangup during a critical elk encounter is setup. If you determine where, when and how you will initiate contact with that oncoming bull elk, you will have all the critically needed elements of proper location(where), timing (when), and ambush site(how) to quickly and humanely kill that bull. However, there is a major problem — and a simple solution — with any bull elk encounter.

The Major Problem

A rutting bull elk comes forward for one of three reasons: to find the cow that's been calling to him, to confront an adversary, or out of curiosity. These are the situations that the bowhunter has

With the aggressive setup, the hunter bugles, then moves forward to an ambush spot about 30 yards ahead. The bull will then pass by as it walks toward the calling location.

created from his cow calling, brush raking, or bugling. While it is true that a bull elk in rut tends to be a bit less wary of danger, a rutting bull elk is not a stupid animal.

Anything in front of him that is unnatural will trigger his cautious instinct. When a bull hangs up just out of bow range, you've probably created some unnatural condition that caused the bull to stop short. Why else would he come forward for a hundred yards or more and then suddenly stop? Hey, it happens to me too! Usually, I can identify my undoing and learn from it, but with a wild animal, sometimes you just have to shrug your shoulders and move on.

However, I have identified improper setups as the leading cause of my failings. Specifically, it has to do with improper positioning. That bull is coming forward looking for another elk. If he approaches the area where the calling has been coming from, but sees no elk, he instinctively hangs up. I also wonder if not finding his adversary where he expected to see him, might signify to a bull that his cowardly challenger had slipped away rather than face him, and the bull might be satisfied to stomp off.

The Simple Solution

The obvious solution to the problem of a bull elk hanging up is to shoot the oncoming bull while he is approaching the area where the calling came from. Sounds impossible, doesn't it? You can't be in two different places at the same time, or can you?

Yes you can! There are two methods of ambushing an oncoming bull before he gets to the calling site. The first, and most common method, is double teaming. The second method is an aggressive one-man setup.

Double Teaming

Probably the best way to waylay an oncoming bull elk is with a two man team. With this method, one hunter is the caller and the other is the hunter. The hunter usually sets up on the near side of an opening where the bull is coming from. The caller stays back about 40 yards, or on the far side of the opening were he can stay well hidden.

The caller then begins working the bull. The oncoming elk approaches the edge of the opening and hesitates while searching the area ahead for the other elk. The shooter then has a perfect shot at the unsuspecting bull. It sounds foolproof, but it's not.

Even with the two-man team, there is a host of things to consider before the caller begins working the bull. First, the two men must get close to the bull without being detected. Two men are an awful lot of erect human bodies stumbling around in the woods, and it's difficult for two guys to be quiet and unseen when they're within 100 yards of a bull.

Second, the shooter must carefully survey the terrain and decide exactly where the bull will come through. It may be a small opening that affords easier walking for the elk, or it may be just a crease in the brush, or a swale. Next, the shooter must be aware of the wind direction and set up in a well concealed ambush site with the wind in his favor.

However, the biggest problem facing a two-man team is communication. Remember, the caller and the shooter may be anywhere from 20 to 50 yards apart, and when a bull is nearby, it's darn near impossible to communicate. And believe me, it's critically important to know what the other guy is thinking.

An incident with a client several years back painfully illustrates what can happen when the caller and shooter aren't operating on the same frequency. On that particular hunt, I was guiding a man from Wisconsin in the Bitterroot Mountains of western Montana. An hour after daybreak on the second day of the hunt, we encountered a bugling bull about 400 yards away on the far side of a dense stand of timber.

We quickly moved forward for a radical challenge. I set the client up behind a small fir sapling about 25 yards from a main game trail that emerged from the timber into a small opening on the left side of the sapling. I scooted back about 40 yards to the far side of the opening and hid behind a mountain maple bush.

At the sound of my bugling challenge, the bull immediately responded. His answering bugle ripped through the cool mountain air and sent a shiver of anticipation up my spine. I bugled again, and the bull answered. The elk was moving toward my client, and I began to hear an occasional snap of a tree twig.

Then I saw his mighty rack weaving through the thick growth of trees. Everything looked perfect, but when the bull was about 40 yards from my client's position, he hopped over a blown down tree and continued forward, angling to the right. It became obvious that he would pass by my client on the right side of the sapling instead of the left.

I watched in growing amazement as the bull came ever closer to the sapling, but the man didn't change his stance. The elk was almost upon him. The guy was hunkered down, bow up and ready, but he was pointing in the wrong direction!

I made several wild gestures, but my client continued to stare intently at the trail to the left. The bull passed by the sapling, and I whistled a warning, which got both the elk and hunter looking at me. I jerked my thumb violently to the right, but the man thought I meant the hunt was over and we should go.

He then slowly stood up and put the arrow back in the quiver while the bull elk stood broadside watching him no more than 20 yards away. You should have seen the look on that man's face when he glanced over and spotted that bull staring back at him! If it wasn't so comical, I would have cried!

It's a good idea to discuss communication before an encounter with a bull elk. The thing to remember is that the shooter is usually hidden until the bull passes by. He can't afford to expose himself, so the caller who is set back up to 50 yards must keep track of the bull and give some sort of audible signal if the bull changes direction.

The Aggressive Setup

The aggressive setup is my choice for an elk encounter. It is what I desire when I pursue the bull elk in rut — a one-on-one confrontation between a man with nothing more than a sharp stick trying to kill an angry beast that may weigh up to a half ton. Wow! I get excited just writing about it.

Obviously, the aggressive elk hunter cannot be in two different places at the same time, but he can make the bull think its adversary is somewhere beyond the ambush site. As I move in on a rutting bull to challenge him, I carefully study the landscape for the logical route that the bull will travel through. After I identify the place he'll probably move through, I quickly check the wind direction and look around for a good bush or tree for an ambush site. In just a few seconds, I've decided the where, when and how of my critical encounter.

With that done, I nock an arrow and tighten my chinstrap, so to speak, because all hell is about to break loose! I usually take a deep breath to calm my nerves and then bugle. Even while the echo of my bugle is still ringing through the mountains, I'm scurrying forward to my ambush spot.

It usually takes the startled bull a few seconds to register the fact that a challenger has invaded his domain. But let me warn you, I've had bulls come stomping forward immediately without bothering to bugle, and I barely had time to raise my bow before they were right in front of me!

But usually, the bull will respond with a furious challenging bugle and wait to hear if his ears were playing tricks on him. Now what? You've already moved forward from that first bugling spot! The trick here is to "throw" your bugle to make the bull think your answering bugle is coming from the original spot.

With the aggressive setup, the hunter bugles, then moves forward to an ambush spot about 30 yards ahead. The bull will then pass by as it walks toward the calling location.

My bugle is carried slung over my shoulder, with the mouthpiece under my armpit and the end tucked behind my back. Without taking my eyes off the bull's location, I'll tone down the volume and bugle with the grunt tube in that position so that the sound is actually coming out behind me. This "throwing" of my bugle makes the bull think his adversary is calling from somewhere behind my position.

The bull stomps forward, headed for the location where he thinks the other bull is. Theoretically, I then shoot him. Sometimes it works that way, and sometimes pandemonium reigns! Bull elk are big animals, and they sometimes have their own ideas about the best travel route.

At times, I've had to scoot left or right like a tunnel rat virtually under an advancing bull's nose to get into proper shooting position. And yes, at times I've been "caught" scooting. But more often than not, a preoccupied bull will not catch careful movement by a bowhunter who stays low. That's why I love that hated alder brush in Idaho and that Colorado oak brush. True, you can't see well in the stuff, but neither can an advancing bull, and you can often change your position virtually in front of the bull's nose!

There is a great deal of satisfaction in a successful aggressive elk encounter. You alone did all the planning. You did your own calling. You chose the perfect setup and ambush, and finally, you put that arrow in the perfect place to insure a quick, humane kill.

That's also why I'll stick with my opinion that when everything goes right, it's hard for me to trivialize such an awesome encounter with so precious a wilderness animal by saying the bull was too small. At 10 yards broadside, every bull elk looks like a worthy trophy to me!

A hunter who is mentally prepared will be able to stay calm and perform the simple chore of shooting an arrow into a passing bull's chest.

Chapter 5

Mental Preparation For An Elk Encounter

My client on one particular elk hunt was a man of great influence. He was the president of a large computer firm in Chicago, and he had total authority over a large number of people. With the slightest nod of his head, he could decide the fate of a man's career. He was also a powerfully built man who showed up for his hunt in great shape.

He was a no-nonsense guy who had done his homework before his bowhunt for elk. He'd studied all the correct publications and was carrying all the right archery gear for killing an elk. He'd read several of my elk hunting articles in Bowhunter magazine, so I guess he figured I must know what I was doing.

The only little problem the man had was with control. He had to have it! Twice, on the first day of the hunt, he ended up leading the way. Whereupon, I had to remind him that if he led, I'd have to refund his guided hunt fee!

The man had also read extensively about the bull elk and how to hunt it. Those first few days, we had a few very interesting conversations about how we would hunt a particular bugling elk. And I have to admit, the guy had an excellent grasp on almost all aspects of elk hunting except one.

That became obvious one morning when we encountered a very agitated bachelor bull. The angry elk bugled constantly from a stand of dense timber along the edge of an old burn. We moved in quickly for a radical challenge, but I had to hold up for a few minutes while my client debated with me the correct approach. Hmm!

Finally, he agreed that my way had possibilities. With that laborious chore accomplished, we slipped to within 100 yards of the timber stand. Even at that distance, we could hear brush breaking and limbs snapping as the rangy elk challenged every tree and sapling in his domain.

I positioned my client behind a small clump of fir trees that looked ideal for a downwind ambush spot if the bull came forward through a narrow opening to his left. I then scooted back about 30 yards and hunkered down behind a small spruce tree. To my chagrin, the man decided he knew a better ambush spot and moved about 15 yards to his right. Hmm!

With great anticipation, I emitted a long, high-pitched bugle. The area where the bull had been making noise became deathly silent. Suddenly, the five-point bull broke cover at a trot about 80 yards away. His head was thrown back and he was bugling furiously.

The bull came fast and hard, and he didn't stop until he lowered his head to ram a three-inch diameter lodgepole tree. The bull began viciously attacking the poor tree, and my client would have had a perfect 20 yard shot — if he had stayed where I had positioned him.

The bull then bugled and trotted in a semicircle before ramming his antlers into the brush and tearing out a huge gouge of dirt and huckleberry bushes. It was a magnificent and awesome display of rutting bull elk bravado. The fury and frantic pace of the bull's movements were classic rutting behavior of a frustrated bachelor bull.

Finally, the bull quit gesturing and stood broadside about 15 yards in front of my client. The elk extended his neck and bellowed a huge bugle that shook the ground. My client drew back and put an arrow about two feet over the bull's rump. The startled bull trotted forward about 15 yards, picked up human scent and bolted.

After the forest quieted down, I approached a very shaken man who trembled from head to toe. He had finally encountered someone he couldn't control. I half expected some kind of self-righteous excuse, but the man showed his true mettle when he looked me in the eye and said, "I really blew it! I don't even remember drawing back the bow. I don't even think I aimed!"

My status rose a notch or two in that man's eyes after that, and we had several very enjoyable philosophical conversations about mental preparation for an elk hunt. Unfortunately, he spaced out again when it counted and missed a 30 yard shot at another five point bull before his hunt ended.

He's not alone. At least he released an arrow! Twice, I've had hunters watch gape-mouthed as a rut-crazed bull elk stomped by within easy killing range, and they never even brought the bow up! That's the way a rampaging bull elk affects a good hunter who may not have hunted or killed anything bigger than a whitetail deer.

Preparing mentally for a close range encounter with an aggressive animal of impressive size should be at the top of the list of preseason priorities for a hunter planning an elk hunt. There are several ways to accomplish this. Some are as old as the dawn of man, the hunter, and some are the result of modern technology.

The first hurdle that a prospective elk hunter must get over is the shock of a sudden point-blank encounter with a rutting bull elk. Unless you've been 20 yards from one of these animals, you have no idea how physically impressive they can be. A mature bull elk may

Preparing mentally for a close range encounter with an aggressive bull elk should be at the top of the list of preseason priorities for any first-time elk hunter.

The inner man still possesses that fearless hunter's spirit that put him at the top of the food chain. The modern man just has to dig deep inside of himself and find it.

weigh upwards to 1,000 pounds, and his massive antlers may have a spread of four feet or more.

No matter how physically or mentally strong a man may be, he is finally confronted with an animal that is bigger and stronger. And instead of being intimidated, it does the intimidating!

Add to that the surly, vocal nature of a rut-crazed bull elk, and you can understand how an archer who has never even seen an elk — could go into shock! For that matter, resident archers don't do that well,either. I know of many guys born and raised in the mountains of Montana who kind of go blank when a big bull comes stomping forward looking for them.

I firmly believe that the inner man still possesses that fearless hunter's spirit that put us at the top of the food chain. In ages past, man faced formidable odds and great danger when he encountered ferocious fanged beasts during the hunt. But his keen intelligence turned the slightest advantage into victory, and his determination to stand and face his adversary pushed this puny creature we call "man" to the top of the list of the most deadly creatures roaming the face of the earth.

An encounter with a rampaging bull elk is indeed a primal confrontation not unlike the conflicts our ancestors faced. Think about it. The modern bowhunter is facing an angry animal of superior strength and power armed with nothing more than a sharp stick. And it is the archer who digs deep within his spirit and draws from that primal reservoir of fortitude who ultimately performs the deadly task before him with razor sharp effectiveness.

It is this confrontation that I desire when I go elk hunting. Hey, I work and earn money! As good as elk meat is, I really don't need it to survive. And there are already enough elk racks in my garage gathering dust. Instead, I yearn for this intense primeval confrontation between man and beast that forces me to draw from that well of humanity that is pure predator — the dilated pupils; the short choppy breaths; the sudden keenness of instinctive reactions — these are the signs of an adrenalin-charged man on the cutting edge of predation. In the business world, or in the Rocky Mountains, that is exactly what we are — a predator.

As dumb as it may seem, start by eyeing up domestic stock, such as horses or cows in a field. Get close to an animal who's size and potential power are much greater than yours, and feel that animal's daunting physical presence. Get used to that feeling until your courage begins to assert itself. Look it in the eye and visualize it as a bull elk, and then zero in on a spot about six inches behind its shoulder where you "shall and you will!" put that arrow.

If possible, go to a zoo and study the elk there. Watch how they walk, and become accustomed to the aura of the bull elk. Study his movements, and rivet your eyes on the spot behind his shoulders. In your mind, raise your bow as the elk walks by, draw when he turns broadside, and when his front shoulder rolls forward — RELEASE! We have a herd of three bulls and four cow elk in a three acre pen at a tourist stop near my home. In August, I spend many hours intently studying the bulls. Over and over again, I mentally draw and release as a bull walks by. It is truly a labor of love to do this exercise.

Preparing mentally for your hunt by looking at a horse in a field, or a penned elk, is one thing. A rampaging bull elk is another thing altogether. There's a world of difference between the two, for

Video target systems, such as this Dart Target System, allow an archer to experience the excitement of a close range encounter with a huge bull elk long before his hunt takes place.

one is fantasy and one is reality. In the past that transition had been a real problem for first-time hunters, but modern technology allows us to experience that adrenalin high of a frantic confrontation with a rut crazed bull elk long before archery season begins.

An ingenious new target shooting system produced by Dart International of Denver, Colorado, utilizes an 8X10 foot laser sensitive video screen upon which are displayed a series of life-size animals moving through the forest. When the archer hits an animal, the figure freezes, and the animal's vital area is outlined in red, with the arrow's impact point highlighted to show the shooter exactly how well, or how poorly, he shot.

As a result of this wonderful target system, you can now experience the drama of the hunt in the comfort of your local pro archery shop long before your planned hunt, as a huge angry bull elk emerges from the trees and bellows out a challenge before raking his mighty antlers on a tree.

If there isn't a Dart Target System nearby, harass your local archery shop to get one! I'm proud to say that as an employee of

Stoney-Wolf Video Productions, I videod many of the target scenes on the current Dart elk target disk.

A close range encounter between an archer and a charging bull elk is truly a confrontation as old as man. It is the timeless conflict pitting the ferocious wild beast against the predatory instincts of the animal we call man. Early man stood up to the challenge, and you can too!

An experienced elk hunter uses a combination of bow, arrows and broadheads that will quickly and humanely kill a bull elk.

Chapter 6

The Perfect Elk Archery Outfit

A phone call I received recently from a frustrated archer is typical of a disturbing reoccurrence I've been hearing the past few years concerning elk archery gear. The man was using a very expensive hunting outfit that probably cost upwards to a thousand dollars. He'd gone to his local pro shop and told the owner that he was going on an elk hunt and wanted the perfect elk archery outfit.

What he received was a dazzling, impressive high tech bow with overdraw, ultralight arrows and Space Age broadheads. As luck would have it, he got (in his opinion) a reasonable shot at a four-point bull. The elk stood broadside at about 50 yards and he put the arrow in the middle of the elk's chest.

There was a blood trail to follow, but the chore dragged on for hours as he followed the wounded elk for a half mile. Twice, he saw the animal at a distance and was able to put his binoculars on the elk. Sure enough, there was a gaping wound a bit high in the chest area. Eventually, the man lost the elk in a boggy thicket.

Thinking that I must be the reincarnation of Houdini, he expected me to explain why he didn't kill that elk! I told him, "I don't know exactly why, but I can tell you several things that went wrong. For one thing, you shot at that elk from too far away." Whereupon we engaged in a sometimes-tense conversation about proper shooting range.

His opinion was the standard B.S. about every archer shooting to the limit of his ability. For some guys, that limit might be 30 yards, but for him, it was 60 yards. I countered, "Then why did you wound that elk at 50 yards? If your opinion is accurate, you should

It doesn't matter whether he uses high tech or traditional archery gear, a true sportsman makes sure his outfit will perform.

have killed it, but you didn't, so it would seem reasonable to conclude that you did something very wrong, especially since you swear you saw the wound in a place that should have killed any elk."

He became very quiet for a while and finally mumbled, "I guess you're right. What did I do wrong?" We then proceeded to engage in a fruitful conversation that I believe opened the guy's eyes, but only after he'd opened his mind.

There are many bows, arrows and broadheads to choose from today. That's the good news. The bad news is that some don't kill very well, and some don't kill elk at all. The choice of archery gear that an elk hunter will use to hunt a bull elk is, in my opinion, taken far too lightly. As a sounding board for elk archery hunting, I have been hearing far too many horror stories about seemingly adequate archery bows/arrows/broadheads that failed miserably in the field.

Much of this problem I attribute to the polarization of the two major archery factions. On one side, we have the high tech archers who try to solve all their hunting shortcomings by purchasing some new gadget at the archery shop. They have no idea whether or not their high tech gear will function adequately on an elk. And what

Many of the high tech features of a compound bow are actually detrimental to efficient elk killing.

concerns me the most is that I'm not so sure a lot of them care!

On the other side we have the traditionalists who consider themselves to be the elite of the archery world, eschewing the modern trinkets of technology. In fact, many of these traditionalists are at best mediocre hunters with an arrogant, elitist attitude. They consider themselves a step above anyone who uses a compound bow, and make sure that any compound user within hearing knows their opinion. But in fact, many are such poor shots with their stick bows that they should seriously consider taking up the compound bow and using sights!

Do you see what's happened? Each side has lost sight of the first love of archery, and that is the pursuit of the bull elk. While both camps sniff and posture about how great they are, and how inadequate the other side is, the bull elk limp off to an unknown fate. I'm sick of it. These people have no right to hurt these dear, precious elk. It is noble and righteous to pursue and humanely kill an animal, but to gore, tear, wound — and then walk away from a spotty bloodtrail with a simple shrug of the shoulders — enrages me.

A true sportsman pursues the bull elk with bow and arrow

within the limits of the law until he gets to that point in the hunt when he delivers an arrow into the chest of a bull to cause a quick and humane kill. He can use a recurve, longbow, compound or spear. What's the difference? Is there some sort of macabre satisfaction to be derived from wounding an elk, but you at least did it with a recurve? Or a compound? Good grief!

The Perfect Bow
(Compound)

If you choose to use a compound bow, be aware that many of the high tech features touted by manufacturers are actually detrimental to efficient elk killing. A compound bow creates a mechanical advantage that allows an archer to hold less poundage at full draw. Add to that, sights, mechanical releases and 300 feet per second arrow speed, and it gives a newcomer the feeling of invincibility, especially after driving tacks at the local target range.

Lost in this euphoria is the fact that the average compound bow requires at least five seconds to draw and release — far too long for the quick shooting often necessary during a confrontation with a rutting elk. Consequently, the guy who can shoot a three inch group at 40 yards, is horrified when he is off target by two feet at 30 yards — because he rushed his shot! This high tech archery gear is deadly accurate when shot under controlled conditions, but a plucked string on a short, fast compound bow shooting ultralight arrows will zing an arrow up into the trees.

I've killed about half my elk with a compound bow, but I arrived at this sobering fact: I could not expect to kill an elk unless it was within 30 yards. I also got tired of fighting the tuning problem, bent sight pins, and the extra weight. Since I couldn't shoot an elk unless it was close, I decided to go back to the simplicity of a recurve bow. I have not tuned my recurve in six years of use. In fact, I do nothing to make the arrows fly straight — they just do.

However, I understand that everyone is different. In fact, I have a bad shoulder that was injured in a logging accident, and I wouldn't be surprised if I was back to shooting a compound bow again in a few years. No big deal. I'll still enjoy the elk hunt just as much.

The perfect compound bow can be just about any

configuration that you prefer, but you must be able to draw and release it in three seconds. That is the rule of thumb that I use with all the compound users who seek my counsel. In fact, that's the identical criteria I used when I shot a compound bow. I used a rear peep sight and pin sights, and I quickly recognized the need to simplify my gear to become more practical.

As a result, I became deadly accurate shooting within three seconds at ranges up to 25 yards. Beyond that, I needed five or even six seconds, so I avoided those shots. You should do the same. The nature of an encounter with a rutting bull elk is such that the critters won't stand still for five or six seconds. My suggestion for a minimum draw weight on a compound bow would be 60 pounds.

(Recurve Bow)

A recurve bow shot at short range does not insure an elk kill. Somewhere along the line, the traditionalists have gotten the mistaken notion that any recurve bow of 45 pound pull minimum will kill an elk if the range is less than 20 yards. That is simply not true. Any

The author's choice of the perfect elk archery outfit is a Palmer recurve bow, 600 grain cedar arrows (including point), and Magnus broadheads.

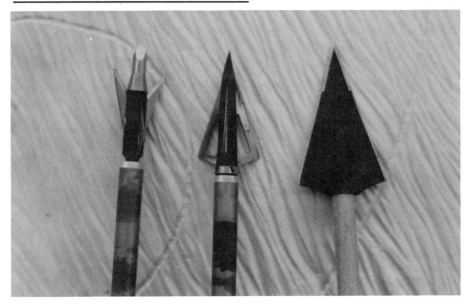

Three common types of broadheads; from left to right, movable blade, presharpened chisel point, and cut-on-contact Magnus broadhead.

arrow, whether it is shot from a recurve or compound, must penetrate an elk's chest deep enough to puncture both lungs.

Consequently, a recurve of sufficient pull is necessary, and here is where the recurve or longbow issue gets muddy. All traditional bows are not the same. Two bows of equal pound pull may have as much as 30 fps difference in arrow speed. We know that arrow speed of a given arrow weight governs penetration, so any traditional shooter should seek out those bows that shoot fast.

Unfortunately, the makeup of a traditional bow has a great impact on its performance. A mass produced bow that sells for only $100 often shoots like a club, while a custom make bow crafted by a bowyer outshoots that cheap bow by 30 fps, but the darn thing costs $600!

Obviously, a happy medium is needed. There are some very good manufactured bows that are quite efficient, such as the line of recurve bows offered by Bear Archery. I have one and swear by it.

The perfect bow for me is a Palmer recurve set at 65 pounds for my draw. The Palmer bow is made to accommodate the fast-flight string. These strings have no stretch to them, so they put a lot more pressure on the limbs. However, a bow made to use a fast-flight string will shoot like it has five pounds more pull weight. Consequently, my 65 pound pull Palmer keeps up with a 70 pound recurve using a dacron string that stretches. My Palmer bow shot through a chronograph shoots a 650 grain arrow at 201 fps. That's hot!

The Perfect Arrow

Stay away from ultra light shafts for elk. After investigating many woundings of elk, I have come to the conclusion that a heavier weight arrow is necessary for elk. I realize that energy is directly attributable to arrow speed, but that equation is one of simple energy production. It does not take into account vector forces created when heavy muscle or bone is encountered.

After closely studying two apparent dead-center chest shots on elk this past year when archers had used ultralight shafts, I have concluded that the shafts, flying at about 300 fps, encountered a rib and were thrown off to the extent that they actually ricocheted up into the shoulder area. In other words, the heavy mass of an elk made the lightweight arrows glance off course and not enter both lungs, even though it appeared from the archer's viewpoint that the shafts had zipped right through the elk.

My suggestion is that you use whatever type of shaft material you want. Cedar, maple, aluminum, graphite — whatever. Just make sure your bare shaft, without broadhead, weighs in at about 500 grains. That will quickly eliminate several of the more modern shafts.

The Perfect Broadhead

When it comes to broadheads, it's a jungle out there. There is a dizzying array of heads that beckon the prospective archer with hype and extraordinary claims. Most of these heads have no proven track record for doing the job on elk and should be avoided.

I've spoken with concerned guides and outfitters about broadheads, and every one of them has several horror stories to tell about hunters who used broadheads that simply could not do the job on an elk. In fact some outfitters will come right out and ban the use of certain broadheads that have failed.

After speaking with many expert elk hunters, plus guides, I

have come to a few conclusions. The compound user should choose a simple three or four blade head with stationary blades that cut on impact. In the past, that was just about impossible, but in recent years, several broadhead manufacturers have offered a line of cutting edge heads just for the elk hunter who uses high tech archery gear.

My choice for the perfect broadhead is a cutting edge two blade. There really is no reason to use a multiple blade head. A two-blade broadhead that slices into an elk's chest will cause a quick, humane death.

A two blade broadhead also provides deeper penetration. My friend, Paul Brunner, told me that Barry Wensel has recently begun using two-blade broadheads, and Barry said his arrows now penetrate an average of about six inches deeper. This penetration advantage of the two blade broadhead allows an archer with physical limits to use a bow with a few pounds less pull.

Conclusion

The perfect elk archery outfit will be a bow that allows an archer to draw and release an arrow in three seconds. The perfect shaft will weigh about 600 grains with broadhead, enough mass to not glance off a rib. And the broadhead will cut on impact and not stop until both lungs are penetrated.

You are on your own to pick and choose the bells and whistles. Just make sure when you come out here to hunt elk that your elk hunting outfit is made to kill an elk.

Chapter 7

Ten Mistakes Elk Hunters Make

There are errors made during a hunt that often spell the difference between victory and defeat. At times, these errors are very obvious, but sometimes the mistakes are more subtle and need to be explained by experienced elk hunters. The 10 most common mistakes of elk hunters fall into that slot. Some of the mistakes are obvious, while other mistakes tend to be more subtle errors made by most hunters who have trouble killing elk at close range.

Ignorance of Elk

A man from New Jersey stopped in our local archery shop on his way to go archery elk hunting in Idaho. He was within 60 miles of his hunting camp, and he still had not seen a live elk. The shop owner joked to him about bugling, and the hunter had no idea that bull elk bugled! It seems inconceivable with all the hunting videos available today that a man would embark on his dream hunt for elk without even knowing what one looked or sounded like.

Before your first elk hunt, read everything available on elk. And not just hunting books, either. The elk is a fantastic animal, and anyone who hunts elk should consider themselves fortunate to experience a very special outdoor event that most men only dream about.

Read up on the biology of the animal. I would suggest an excellent book titled, *"The Elk of North America"* by Stackpole Books. This is a semi-academic book which contains a great amount of biology that will help you understand the animal you're hunting.

Learn about the type of feed that elk like. Are they browsers or grazers, or both? Do they have a feed to bed cycle like whitetails?

Do bull elk rut only after frosty weather? These are a few of the tantalizing questions that you should have answered before your hunt.

I attribute any success I've had with elk to an in-depth understanding of the animal. When a bull rakes his antlers, or seeks cover, or quits bugling, I know why he is acting that way, and I'm ready to counter his moves because of this knowledge of the life of the elk. Take some time during the off season to browse through the books stores and libraries and gain as much knowledge as you can about this very interesting animal.

Poor Physical Conditioning

When I was a licensed outfitter, I always stressed physical conditioning. I informed clients that their success during the hunt would be directly proportionate to their physical conditioning. This was no idle quip, either. Most of the men who bowkilled elk were in good shape and were able to keep up with me when quick movement was necessary.

In the *Radical Elk Hunting Strategies* book, I related several instances when clients had only to cover ground at a trot for maybe a couple hundred yards to be in perfect ambush position when the elk came by, but those men were not in shape for any rigorous activity, and they just couldn't move fast enough.

Another fallacy about physical conditioning that I hear a lot from sportsmen concerns elk hunting in the Southwest. They tell me that they will be hunting the bull pine or juniper flats of Arizona or New Mexico, so they don't have to get in top physical condition because the terrain is flat.

That is not true. We were on hunts in the famed Valle Vidal trophy area of New Mexico where you had to cover 10-15 miles per day because the elk were scattered far and wide. The terrain varied from rolling to steep. Add to that the fact that the elevation was about 9,000 to 12,000 feet, and you have all the ingredients to sap the strength and spirit from a bowhunter who is not in top physical condition.

However, physical conditioning is not just for the nonresident first-time elk hunter. I live in Montana, and I see far too many local residents who do absolutely nothing to tone their muscles before hunting season. As a result, they never have the stamina to make a

The hunter who understands the basic biology of elk has the best chance for success during his hunt.

A hunter's chances for success during the hunt will be directly proportional to his physical conditioning.

forced march into an area where the bulls are rutting.

Physical conditioning should consist of muscle toning and breathing exercises. Weightlifting is fine for muscle toning, to a degree, but you should concentrate more on active movement-type exercise. Jogging is a great way to improve your wind and tone your legs. Probably the best exercise is bike riding. The leg pumping motion of bike riding closely simulates the pumping motion of mountain climbing. Another good exercise is stair climbing.

Some sportsmen who hunt at high elevation may experience altitude sickness, which produces flu-like symptoms and can ruin a hunt. A good remedy for altitude sickness is Rolaids. Take a half dozen before the morning hunt, and then a few more at midday as needed. The nausea and headaches should subside.

Hunting Where The Elk Aren't

I love elk country and I love the animals, so I spend a lot of time in the mountains before the season begins in Montana. While most guys are tentatively probing areas, trying to locate elk that first morning, I usually have several elk herds already pinpointed. I have killed about 10 bulls the first morning of elk archery season, and some hero-worshipping folks have attributed it to some sort of supernatural elk hunting ability on my part. That is not only dangerous for my ego, but it is also inaccurate. I've killed so many elk the first morning because I knew exactly what sidehill or alpine meadow a particular bull was lurking in, and I would engage him with a radical challenge at dawn on the first morning of the season and kill him. While I was ramming an arrow into a bull's chest a half hour after shooting light, the average bowhunter was still hiking into a place to look for elk. See the difference?

Of course, many elk hunters don't live close to their hunting area. But you can still scout out an area by phoning local sporting good stores, wildlife biologists, and studying topographical maps. If I pinpoint an area in a distant state where statistics show a high elk population and harvest, I'll go to the topo map and quickly pick out areas of prime elk habitat. In mountainous terrain, expect to locate the elk in the upper third of the mountains, where heavy forest begins to give way to subalpine terrain, which contains meadows and timber stands.

In the mountains, look for benches, small lakes, or marshy areas on the map. These are places where the grass is lush and the elk like to live. In the flats of the Southwest, look for marshy areas or small ponds. You'll discover that even the flat areas have low ridges where juniper trees provide elk cover. Expect to find the bulls moving into these refuges to bed down and plan to hunt them.

Don't spend a lot of time in an area where elk do not live. It is a fact that elk do not inhabit an entire area that is considered elk habitat. When I enter a new area, I immediately identify the prime elk habitat. I'll hunt the best looking area that first morning, but if I don't see or hear elk, or spot any tracks, I'm out of there and on to the next likely spot. Usually within a day or two I'm into the elk by using this mobile in-field scouting method.

I've seen far too many nonresident hunters stuck in one draw or ridgetop. They are confused and intimidated by the terrain, so they hunt the same ground every day. The elk may have used that area in the early summer as they moved to the higher prime elk habitat, so there is some old sign. And maybe there is a cow or two still lingering nearby. I've spoken with dejected nonresident bowhunters who hunted hard for seven days without even seeing an elk, while I was into bugling bulls just a few miles away in areas of prime habitat!

Wasting Daylight

Elk are most active during the first two hours of daylight in the morning, and the last hour of light in the evening. This is especially true when the weather is warm. Since the elk usually live a distance away from access roads, far too many hunters burn up valuable hunting time hiking into these prime elk rutting areas.

Many times, I've located rut crazed bulls far back from a road. Next morning, I'd hike for two hours in the dark and be at the downwind edge of the area where the elk were bugling. At first light, I'd go in there, challenge a bull and kill it. By the time I field dressed the carcass and hung the meat, the sun was up and the elk had moved back into their bedding thickets for the day.

As I packed the first load of meat out a couple hours after daybreak, I'd encounter bowhunters just arriving! They'd begun hiking at first light, heard distant bugling and were all excited to get

These well-used trails contain fresh elk tracks. Expect to find elk nearby.

into some rutting bulls, but by the time they got there, they'd burned up all their prime morning hunting hours. This is another reason why many bowhunters are frustrated because bulls will bugle, but not come in to their calling. They are bugling at bedded bulls who are tired and hot and not interested in emerging from their cool bedding thickets.

The one exception to early hunting occurs during the peak of the rut. When the cows go into heat in groups, the bulls go into a rutting frenzy and are active all day. This is a short period of three or four days. Believe me, you'll know when it's happening because the bulls will continue to bugle long after the sun is up, and you'll see cows and bulls moving through the open at midday. At this time, you can expect to engage a rutting bull at any time of day.

Wisconsin resident Bob Mussey encountered an elk herd two miles back from an access road during the peak of the rut. Bob had a great morning hunt and almost killed a bull. His plan was to hunt the early morning hours and then hike back out, but there was so much rutting activity still going on at 9:30 in the morning, that he decided to stay there and work some of the bulls. At 1:30 in the afternoon, at a time of day when you would normally never get a bull to bugle, let alone come in, Bob bugled in a nice five-point bull and killed him with a 25 yard shot.

Too Much Ridgetop Hunting

A ridgetop is the best place to locate bugling bulls, especially in mountainous country. You can bugle off both sides of a ridge and hear any answering elk from a long distance. Ridges are also very easy places to hike because they are free of heavy brush and usually have well traveled trails that make hiking easier.

Unfortunately, those two benefits of ridgetop hunting also become the downfall of many hunters who spend most of their time trying to coax a bull elk to cross a deep draw and come all the way up to them on the ridgetop. Use a ridgetop to locate bugling bulls, or to move from one place to another quickly, but don't spend a lot of time hunting a ridgetop. The elk usually don't spend a lot of time on the top of a ridge. The elk may feed in these open ridgetop areas in the dark, but then drop down into the draws and sidehill thickets to rut and bed down.

Ridgetop hunting is especially a problem for horse hunters. I've seen outfitters with high paying clients who did nothing but ride horses along ridgetops and try to coax bulls to come up to them. It usually doesn't happen. I've also see hunters on foot who just about refused to leave the relatively easy traveling conditions of the ridgetop trails.

In reality, ridgetop hunting is lazy hunting. With that said, I must admit that I will occasionally hunt a ridgetop in the evening. I'll do this to locate bugling bulls and give my tired old leg muscles a break after several punishing hunts.

Generally, if you want to kill a rutting bull, expect to spend most of your actual hunting time down in the heavy brush, deep draws, and timber thickets where elk usually hole up to rut. Sure, use ridgetops to locate bugling bulls and for fast traveling, but then dive off and go after those bugling bulls!

Waiting To Hunt The Peak Rut

The peak rut occurs when the majority of cow elk go into heat. The bulls go crazy and hunting is great. However, the peak rut

The experienced hunter bugles from a ridge to locate elk, but then drops off that ridge to confront a rutting bull.

is a small window that may last no longer than four or five days. As I mentioned, tests by biologists of cow elk harvested during a January crop damage hunt discovered that almost all the cows were impregnated during a six day period. That could mean a guy who hunted only on weekends might totally miss the peak of the rut.

The answer is to plan to also hunt in the early stage of the rut. I've killed most of my elk at this time, before the bulls had been over-bugled and chased by hunters. In the early rut, bulls are very responsive to a radical challenge. In addition, the big herd bulls that are almost impossible to call in when they have harems, are very receptive to a radical challenge early in the rut when they are just beginning to feel frisky and have not yet rounded up a herd of cows.

You can even successfully confront silent bulls in the early rut. During that first week of September, when the bulls may not be bugling much yet, I'll sneak into prime elk habitat and move through areas where elk hang out. I'll bugle and rake the brush, causing a lot of excitement. Many times, I've entered these "elky" areas where no elk had responded to my distant calling. But when I bugled from nearby, I've had bulls respond by bugling back, raking their antlers on the trees, or coming in silently. This is a very exciting way to hunt. It's a real adrenalin rush to bugle and bang the brush with a stick, and then see elk antlers moving above the brush as a bull elk comes forward silently to see what all the commotion is about.

Hunting Only In The Morning

Most of the prime elk habitat is located at least a mile away from access roads or trails. Hunters who hike into these areas usually don't get there on time. They locate the bulls as the elk are moving back to their distant bedding areas. By that time these hunters are tired and hungry, so they head back to camp or their vehicle. In doing that, they have eliminated the evening hunt because most guys are simply not going to hike all the way back to camp, rest up sore muscles, and then hike all the way back into the prime elk rutting areas during the late afternoon heat.

Experienced hunters always plan to stay in the field the entire day. I usually carry a backpack or fanny pack filled with enough

In the early part of the rut, bull elk who don't bugle too often will respond to a hunter's bugling and brush raking.

food, water and a book to tide me over during the midday lull in action. Often times during this midday period, I've heard and seen peak rutting activity beginning and moved right in for a kill. Early in the rut, you can be situated at midday on a comfortable ridgetop and have the bugling bulls pinpointed from the morning's activity and be ready to move in on them when they get up and become active in the evening.

Poor Setup Position During Ambush

This is a big problem among bowhunters who do everything right, and then blow it at the very last second. And the culprit is usually poor setup. The thing to remember during an ambush of an oncoming bull elk is that he is moving forward because he thinks you are an elk. Consequently, he's going to walk directly to the spot where your calling is coming from.

Unless you plan your ambush correctly, the result will be a bull elk standing 15 yards away facing you, but you can't shoot because you have only a poor frontal shot. I don't have enough fingers and toes to count the times other archers have told me about exactly this type of encounter. Eventually, a bull will either see, hear, or become suspicious of the hunter, and retreat.

The key to a successful ambush setup is to get the bull in the broadside position as he passes by looking for you. Survey the immediate area where your ambush will occur and pick out a spot where the bull will have to pass by on his way to an opening where he is sure to stop and survey the open area ahead for the other elk.

Always set up your ambush on the downwind side of a travel lane the bull will move through. Mountain wind currents are especially tricky, so you can't count on a cross wind holding steady, especially as the thermal air currents begin to switch the predominant wind direction from downhill to uphill as the sun heats the air. Poor ambush setup, and specifically poor wind direction, is the culprit for most of my failed elk encounters.

Poor Shot Placement

Whitetail hunters are taught to aim at a deer's chest right along the back line of the leg bone. A deer's shoulder blade is very thin and creates little resistance for a razor sharp arrow. You won't

The key to a successful ambush is to get the bull in the broadside position as he passes by.

get away with that shot on an elk. A bull's shoulders are a mass of heavy bone and muscle that will stop most arrows after only an inch or two of penetration.

However, an elk's chest is much larger than a deer's chest and extends about 18 inches behind the protection of the shoulder blade, so you have a larger lung area to shoot at. You don't have to slip an arrow right along the back of the front leg to hit the lungs. I usually pick a spot on an elk's chest about six inches behind the back line of the foreleg.

That's a perfect spot to dead center the lungs, yet miss the shoulder blade. However, if you are using the proper archery outfit, you can usually punch an arrow through the shoulder blade. On three different occasions, I've been off target a bit and hit the bull in the back part of the shoulder blade, but my razor sharp two-blade broadhead easily sliced through the bone-like cartilage of the shoulder blade and punctured both lungs.

Elk are long-legged animals who moved deceptively fast even walking at a casual pace. Archers have trouble picking a spot to aim at when a fast-moving bull comes stomping past. You can stop a passing bull by cow calling or just saying "Hey." The bull will stop to identify the source of the sound, and you'll have a standing broadside shot.

Inadequate Field Dressing Gear

My friend, George Regan, killed a dandy five-point bull a few years ago. He'd killed several deer during his hunting career, but this was his first elk kill. He was understandably thrilled, but the euphoria quickly left him when he discovered that the bull was so heavy that he could not even roll it on its back to begin field dressing it.

Adding to his woes was the fact that George carried only a large pocket knife to do all the field dressing. George told me, "That hollow elk hair dulled my knife before I even got finished opening up the belly. I had to try to sharpen it on a rock! It took me four hours to field dress that elk, and I was covered from head to toe with blood."

In contrast, it takes me about 45 minutes to completely field dress and hang the elk meat in quarters. (See Chapter 11 for specific instructions.) Never go elk hunting without proper field dressing gear, which should include three sharp knives, a saw, rope, plus heavy duty game bags. Learn how to field dress an animal as large as an elk, and make tentative plans to have someone process the meat when you get it back to civilization. Don't wait until you have all the meat piled in the back of your pickup to start searching for the location of a meat locker.

Bill Krenz says the key to his success with elk is his ability to quickly locate elk in any area he enters.

Chapter 8

Hunting Secrets of the Experts
(Krenz, Jones, Carlton, Brunner, Schuh, Robb)

I am very fortunate to count as my personal friends most of the top elk experts. Names such as Bill Krenz, Larry D. Jones, Wayne Carlton, Paul Brunner, Dwight Schuh and Bob Robb read like a "Who's Who of Elk Hunting." Between them are 100 bull elk kills and a wealth of woodsmanship that has brought them the title of elk expert.

These men have graciously agreed to share their secrets with you to make you a better elk hunter. I asked each man to identify one of the main reasons why he was successful hunting elk. Each expert had something different to say, yet there is also a similarity in their hunting styles. It stands as further proof that experienced hunters find success mainly through determination, resourcefulness, and a willingness to be open to learning something new about elk.

Bill Krenz

The key to success I've had with elk is my ability to find where the elk live. I do a lot of homework because I usually hunt areas far from where I live. When I go into a new area, I aggressively seek out those areas where the elk are supposed to live, such as high country lakes, flat benches, and at the heads of basins.

I'll move through these areas, bugling, glassing and looking for sign. If I don't see anything that gets me excited, I'll leave that area. Elk are animals that like to roam around a lot. They may feed on a sidehill one day and be a couple miles away the next day for no apparent reason. I hunt the same way. I won't spend an extra day tromping over the same area where I found no sign of elk the day before. I'll move a couple miles or five miles to another place that my preseason scouting indicated as elk habitat.

I'm not above breaking camp several days in a row while I seek out those areas where the elk live.

That's one of the big mistakes I see a lot of nonresidents making. They'll move into some picturesque campground that's enjoyable to stay at, and they'll spend their entire hunt roaming through hills that have very few, if any, elk. You have to realize that the West is a very vast expanse of habitat, but most of it is not prime elk habitat. And even in that prime elk habitat, the elk are constantly roaming through it. Just because you find some nice wallows and good feed in a secluded high country basin, that doesn't necessarily mean the elk are there. They may have all followed the herd bull and his harem into another basin. A lot of hunters will spend days hunting a prime elk area for bulls that may be clustered in the next drainage over. That's my key to success. I keep going until I find that secluded spot where the elk are concentrated. Then it's just a matter of using basic elk hunting techniques to bring a bull into bow range.

Larry D. Jones

I try to put excitement into my elk calling. Too many guys blow on their calls and make them sound so lifeless that you can't blame the elk for not answering them. When I move into an area where I know there are elk, I just won't give up calling until I get a response.

Last fall, I met several bowhunters as I hiked into an area who informed me that the area was dead. I knew there were elk in the area because I'd hunted it before, so I moved down the trail a half mile and started bugling and cow calling. Not just here and there. I mean I really got with the program. Before long, the entire area was lit up with bugling bulls.

I'm also not afraid to try any type of call that the elk might respond to. It doesn't matter whether we think it will work or not. Last fall, Dwight Schuh and I were double teaming a couple of bugle shy bulls. I was the shooter, so I was out in front of Dwight. The bulls just weren't responding, even though Dwight was doing a good job of calling.

I decided to try something different, so I started calling with my Screamer mouth diaphragm. For some reason, the high pitch of that call did something for those bulls because they really opened up whenever I used that call.

I'm not so sure a lot of calling isn't a matter of persistence. Last fall, Dwight and I were hunting in Montana, and Dwight was bugling into the head of a basin that looked like prime elk habitat. He wasn't getting any response, so I started bugling. Not once or twice, either. I stared bellowing over and over again. Before long, several bulls were answering my bugles. Of course, Dwight claimed that he'd "primed their pumps before I got started!"

Another thing I won't do is limit myself to any of the old stereotypes about elk calling. For instance, you're not supposed to be able to call in bulls in hot weather, or in the middle of the day. But last fall in Oregon, I called in and killed a nice five-point bull in 90 degree heat in the middle of the day. If you can convince a bull that you are a cow in heat, that bull isn't going to care what the temperature is or what time of day it is.

Larry D. Jones finds lots of success with rutting elk by putting lots of excitement in his calling.

Wayne Carlton

First off, there's no sense coming up with a great hunting technique if you're not hunting where the bulls live. It drives me nuts when I'm hunting hard in a place where there aren't any bulls. I keep moving until I find the elk. That's not always as easy as it sounds, but a guy can generally find out where the elk live by asking around or making a few phone calls. You're never going to get enough directions to pinpoint the exact sidehill where a bull elk lives because the elk like to roam, so you have to do some roaming too.

My calling runs the gamut of sounds. If I'm into rutting bulls, I'll make a few standard cow calls, but then I'll switch to the fighting cow call and become a lot more insistent by really drawing out that fighting cow call. I want to generate some excitement to those elk that are hearing me.

I'm not above trying just about any elk sound to get a bull into range. Sometimes a bull might hang up short of shooting range when I'm cow calling. I'm not afraid to let go with a few bugles in

Wayne Carlton says his aggressive calling technique brings in many bulls within easy killing range.

that situation, and I've had bulls come that extra distance into bow range by bugling after I'd called them in a long ways with cow calls.

You have to get into the flow of things with rutting bull elk. They're excited, unpredictable and vocal. I get charged up just like the bulls and my calling reflects an excited elk, whether I'm cow calling or bugling. I also don't rely on the elk to offer me a killing shot. I feel it's my responsibility to make that killing shot opportunity, and I go about it that way. I do whatever is necessary to get myself into position to make a clean killing shot.

Paul Brunner

I am totally mobile when I hunt elk. I'll cover up to 10 miles roaming through elk country looking for that right bull. Most bull elk will stand their ground when you move in and bugle at them in their back yard. That's what I do. I'll sneak in and then open up with bugling or cow calls. If the bull is small, I cut off contact and I'm headed in the direction of the next bull I heard bugling, maybe in another drainage.

It's not unusual for me to encounter three or four bulls every day at close range in the peak of the rut. I just keep moving until I find a big bull that I want. I want to say right here that I'm not one of those elite trophy hunters, but if I put a high standard on the bull I kill, look at how much fun I have bugling in all those other bulls.

In the course of the season, I'll have a dozen bulls within killing range before I take a big bull. It's not that the others are below my standards. Heck, they're all trophies, in my opinion. It's just that by limiting myself to taking a 300 point or better bull, I have the pleasure of seeing a lot of rutting bulls doing their thing at point-blank range. That's the enjoyment of elk hunting for me.

And believe me, the fun ends when you finally arrow that big bull miles from your vehicle. That's another part of elk hunting that too many lazy guys are missing. I believe elk hunting should be physically difficult. You have to push yourself to get into the country where the elk live, and then you have to find out how it feels to pack out an elk on your back. It's exhausting, but it's all part of the hunt. If you take shortcuts by having other people do things for you, you're going to miss out on a lot of the personal enjoyment of hunting rutting bull elk.

Paul Brunner likes to be mobile and covers up to 15 miles each day in search of big bulls like this one.

I look at lack of mobility as the main problem with most elk hunters. They just don't cover enough ground to get into those rutting bulls who are crazy with rut. And I put a lot of the blame on inadequate footwear. These guys who come out here after elk wear the most awful, heavy boots to hunt in 70 degree weather.

They have boots that are stiff and cumbersome, and they tend to slow down and tire out a guy in a few hours of hiking. Supposedly, these stiff, rock-hard boots will keep a guy's ankles from turning over. I think that's highly overrated as a danger to most guys. The average sportsman has got good strong feet from being outdoors. He doesn't have to put his feet into a virtual cast with laces to keep from spraining his ankles. In fact, I can't ever remember having a hunter turn an ankle while hunting with me.

I wear a light stalking shoe that might weigh a couple of ounces at most. It's made of a rubber bottom to protect the bottom of my feet, and a light canvas upper. I can, and have, gone on long, all-day elk hunts up to 15 miles in these boots without getting sore feet. Heavy boots also make a guy's feet sweat too much. The feet then become soft from the moisture, and that's when you develop blisters.

Dwight Schuh

I believe the key to my success elk hunting is my willingness to hunt under any conditions. Most of the time, conditions aren't perfect. It's either raining or snowing, or the elk are leading you farther and farther from camp, and in order to kill that bull, you have to be willing to follow them.

I know guys who'll quit a promising elk hunt because it starts raining and it gets a little wet. That's why they make rain gear. Most guys are also a little fearful of the big woods, even if they are native westerners. You can't be aggressive if you're worried about getting lost or going hungry.

I carry a large day pack that contains everything I need to camp out overnight if I have to. Too many times, you get in close to the elk at last light, and most guys cut off contact at the very best hunting time because they're afraid to get caught away from camp after dark.

Last fall, Larry D. Jones and I worked a big bull in a dense

Dwight Schuh believes the key to his success is his willingness to hunt under any conditions. His pack contains all the necessities to stay overnight in a spot where the elk are rutting hard.

timbered draw, and it wasn't until the last hour of light before we got close to him. If we were worried about getting back to camp, we would have left that draw for camp. But we were prepared. We went in there and Larry killed the bull. We had plenty of food and water for an overnight camp, plus an overnight shelter, compass and map. We never felt threatened in the least.

I would guess that half the elk I've killed were the result of my day pack. It gives me the freedom to go wherever the elk might be and not worry about getting lost or hungry or cold or spending a night huddled under a tree.

Bob Robb

There are several things that I feel are very important when it comes to locating elk to shoot arrows at today. I think all of these things are very important and can't be separated into high and low priority during an elk hunt.

First off, hunt where the elk are: Most people don't take enough time to do their homework before a hunt, which in this day

Bob Robb is one of the most intelligent elk hunting experts. He cites several important tips, from physical conditioning, to careful calling, to proper archery gear.

of heavy hunting pressure may be more important than basic hunting skills. Call game departments, biologists, foresters, friends-of-friends. You'd be amazed how much I can pinpoint an elk herd from an evening of phone calls.

Use maps before and during the hunt: These maps show potential elk-holding pockets and help you plan your hunt beforehand, and they save you valuable time by preventing you from wandering aimlessly searching for good elk habitat.

Hunt away from the crowds: Even a car hunter can do this. Instead of taking the heavy-used trails into an area, I will often use my maps to find accessible areas between the trailheads. Most of the hunters take the easy trail routes, and the elk know that. The hunters push the elk into pockets between the trails, and I'm there waiting!

Careless calling kills a hunt: Are bulls bugle shy? Does a bear poop in the woods? Rather than try to bugle up a storm, I try to get ahead of the elk by listening to their calling. I'll then circle and wait for them to move in to me. Sure, there are times when I will bugle my guts out, but the timing has to be right. Mostly, I cow call sparingly.

Watch the darn wind: Duh! Too many people watch only wind they can feel, and they don't check currents on windless days. I wear out a couple of butane lighters in a week's elk hunting as I constantly check the wind. And don't just check the wind when you get into elk. Check it constantly to make sure you're hunting into it.

Don't overbow yourself: With today's incredibly efficient compound bows, you don't need a bow that pulls 80 pounds to put an arrow into an elk's chest. Use a bow you can handle and use razor-sharp broadheads. Get good with it and make sure you can shoot it from odd positions with a minimum of body motion.

Wear quiet clothes: Only two kinds of outerwear are acceptable to me — wool and fleece. Period. Also use soft-soled boots, don't have any exposed metal to bang around, and be sure to cover up the hands and face, as well as paint or tape over shiny bow parts.

Take enough time: Anyone who can consistently kill a bull over a weekend is related to the good Lord and should buy lottery tickets. Most hunters take only five days for an elk hunt. If I can't spend at least a week, and preferably 10-14 days, I feel like I am severely handicapped. The more time you spend in the woods, the better your chances of finding elk and getting a shot.

Get in shape: Elk Hunting is as physically demanding as any type of hunting a person will ever do. I've found that, simply stated, the more ground you can cover in search of the elk, the better your chances of killing one. That means covering 10 to 20 miles a day for a week or 10 days in high altitude mountain country carrying hunting gear. This last point cannot be emphasized enough!

Chapter 9

Some "Really Different" Elk Hunting Methods

There are specific behavioral traits that elk have which form the basis for most of our hunting methods. The radical elk hunting method is an outgrowth of these behavioral traits. So, too, is this book. However, we should never be so vain or narrow-minded that we close our minds to a new hunting method, no matter how unusual it may appear — at least until we give it a try.

There are some new, "really different" elk hunting methods emerging that may prove to be an alternative to the standard two-man or one-man ambush of a bugling bull elk. Some of these really different methods take advantage of improvements in technology, while others take advantage of certain elk behavioral traits that may have been overlooked by traditional elk hunters.

Elk Decoy

I believe that this new method will take the elk archery hunting fraternity by storm over the next few years. I had identified the need to get an oncoming bull to focus his attention on an area beyond the bowhunter. But in the past, there were no good elk decoys, so I never even attempted decoying.

Now all that's changed. Mel Dutton, the maker of the famous Mel Dutton antelope decoy, has done it again with a very light, collapsible, yet life-size and amazingly life-like cow decoy. Experimental? Not hardly! Already good success has been reported by hunters and guides using the cow decoy.

Some hardened elk hunters might snort and quip, "I'd like to see you try to pack an elk decoy back where I hunt!" The cow decoy

The use of an elk decoy will take the elk archery fraternity by storm over the next few years.

weighs only eight pounds and is fitted into a snug backpack. I'm totally sold on this Dutton decoy. So much so that we will be doing an elk hunting video with the Dutton cow decoy this fall, and I fully expect to record an elk kill on film using the cow decoy.

Pennsylvania resident Robert Ehle was made a believer in the Dutton cow decoy this past fall when he hunted with a guide in Colorado. BACA Outfitters had already scored on several bulls using the cow decoy before Robert arrived for his hunt, but he still wondered how this revolutionary hunting method would work when he and his guide approached an old clearcut.

They spotted several bulls below them. One bull began raking his antlers on a tree, so Robert started moving in on him, but the bull stopped raking before Robert could get into range. In the meantime, his guide had set up the cow decoy and began cow calling from behind it. The bull looked up at the sounds of the cow calls, spotted the decoy, and made a beeline for it. Robert was out of position when the bull passed by, and he watched in utter frustration as the bull stomped to within 10 feet of the cow decoy before finally walking past it up the mountainside.

Robert Ehle with his Colorado bull that was lured in with the help of a cow elk decoy.

The men set up a more proper ambush, with Robert this time in good shooting position. The guide began cow calling, and the bull immediately started back down the mountain toward the decoy. As the bull approached Robert's hiding place, the bull's eyes were glued to the cow decoy. Robert shot the elk at a distance of eight yards and soon claimed a dandy five-point bull.

You can two-man it with a cow decoy by placing the shooter off to the downwind side of a bull's travel lane, and placing the caller behind the decoy. As a bull comes in, the caller can even wiggle the decoy a bit to give it some life. The Dutton decoy can even have a peep hole installed so the caller won't have to expose himself to keep track of the oncoming bull.

You can even one-man it with the cow decoy. Place the decoy in an opening that affords the hunter a good downwind ambush spot. The hunter then sets up and begins cow calling. Normally, a bull that steps into an opening and hears a cow call off to the side is not going to go forward, but, with the cow decoy setting out there, he will focus all his attention on the decoy and not concern himself with where the calling seems to be coming from.

The sound of antlers clacking together often gets the attention of a nearby bull.

I believe the cow decoy will prove to be the "missing link" for elk hunting in the open terrain of the great southwestern elk states of Arizona, New Mexico and Colorado. Much of the elk habitat is moderately open to sparse. Oftentimes, the hunter is hunkered down behind a small juniper or sagebrush, and an oncoming bull quickly grows suspicious when he approaches an open area where calling had been coming from, but sees no elk for hundreds of yards of open terrain. The cow decoy would act as a magnet, and I fully expect to hear some great success stories concerning this relatively new hunting method.

Rattling For Elk

Kind of sounds like snipe hunting, doesn't it? However, there has been a smattering of success stories coming back to me from hunters who have successfully used elk antlers to entice a rutting bull into range. An incident that I witnessed in Canada's Banff National Park this past fall firmly convinced me that rattling in elk has great potential.

I'd been videoing a mean old herd bull that had already treed me twice, so I decided to get away from the angry bull for a while. He was having enough problems with the other elk anyway. Twice, he'd put the run on two satellite bulls who'd tried to sneak in on his cows.

I followed the satellite bulls to a small meadow about 100 yards away from the herd bull. The two bachelor bulls squared off and began pushing and shoving at each other. Their locked antlers ground and clacked ominously as they dug in and strained for dominance. (If you shoot the Dart elk target system, you'll see these two bulls sparring in one target scene.)

I noticed that when the satellite bulls began clacking their antlers together, the herd bull began bugling up a storm. I was concentrating on videoing the sparring bulls when a movement behind me caught my eye. I almost fainted when I spotted the big herd bull, stomping toward me. Fortunately, he ignored me. He lowered his mighty rack and routed the two bachelor bulls.

And then it hit me. The sound of those bulls' antlers clacking had pulled the herd bull away from his harem of cows to investigate the commotion just out of his view.

My friend, Bob Robb, told me that he killed a huge Montana bull a few years back by using a variation of rattling. He'd encountered a dandy bull that would not come all the way in to his bugling. He was frustrated when he pulled back from the bull that evening. The next morning, on the way in to the draw where he'd last encountered the bull, Bob found a single shed antler.

Immediately, a light bulb went off in his head. He moved in as close as he dared to the bugling bull and began taunting him with his own calling. He banged the brush, and then spotted the bull looking over in his direction from about 100 yards away. Bob then stuck the single antler over the top of a small fir tree. The big bull went berserk! He came in fast and hard, and Bob put an arrow deep into his chest. Bob told me, "I believe this whole antler and rattling thing has real possibilities."

The one problem with elk antlers is their weight. I intend to use a smallish four point-rack for rattling this fall. I'll cut off the long sweeping dagger points to lessen the weight and make the rack easier and quieter to pack. Don't be surprised if you don't see an article by me about rattling elk in *Bowhunter* magazine in the near future.

Bugle & Stalk

This method of elk hunting is an exciting takeoff from the standard spot & stalk method so popular with mule deer hunters. I know of several hunters who specialize in moving silently in on a bull, especially the hard-to-hunt herd bull. This is one of Paul Brunner's favorite methods of getting even with herd bulls.

Paul told me, "Recently, we had a herd bull that just wouldn't budge from his cows, and every time we moved forward to confront him, he'd move his harem away. Finally, we used the bugle & stalk method. I stayed back and began bugling constantly at the herd bull. The bull would answer every one of my bugles, but stayed put. So did I, but my partner didn't!

"He carefully moved forward. It took him over an hour to stalk the last 100 yards because he had to avoid detection by the cows. He finally got a good 20 yard shot at the bull and killed him."

Paul added, "The bugle and stalk method is a real challenge. Those cows are ever-alert and sharp eyed, and it's a real

Walter Naki with his dandy bugle & stalk bull.

accomplishment to be able to slip past all those watchful eyes and arrow the herd bull."

Some archers who hunt alone also use the spot and stalk method. Idaho resident Jim Prescott told me, "I haven't bugled in a bull in four years, but I've killed a nice bull every year. Here in North Idaho where I hunt, the brush is so thick that it's sometimes useless to bugle in a bull because you can hardly see 10 yards to shoot.

"I listen for the elk to bugle and then slip in on him. The bull's bugling keeps him pinpointed for me, plus the bull makes a lot of noise as he moves through the thick brush. And the brush hides me from his view. If he hears me stepping on brush, he thinks I'm just another elk and may even come forward to join me. It's a very tense, exciting, and rewarding way to hunt rutting elk. I actually like stalking elk more than bugling them in."

Chicken Feathers

The folks at Brigade Quartermaster, who manufacture ASAT 3D camouflage, may be a bit chagrined by our tongue-in-cheek

ASAT camouflage in 3D pattern works great in the open Southwest elk terrain.

name, chicken feathers, for their new three dimensional camouflage, but they can't complain about our compliments for this innovative new camo pattern.

ASAT 3D camouflage uses an indestructible no-noise, soft nylon material sewn onto a strong mesh fabric. The nylon is free to flutter and move in the breeze and breaks up a human's form so well that it's very difficult to spot a stationary hunter wearing this pattern.

A guide for U.S. Outfitters gave the ASAT 3D its comical name when he inspected the outfit during a New Mexico bowhunt and commented that it worked very well, but it puffed a guy out and made him look like he was covered with camouflaged "chicken feathers."

ASAT 3D is more than unique. It works! I've seen guys spend thousands of dollars on a trophy elk hunt in the open southwestern states. But then these guys showed up in dark green camouflage that may have been expensive, but it made them stand out like dark green blobs to the elk. More than once, I witnessed oncoming elk spook when they spotted a green-clad bowhunter trying to hide behind a dusty gray sagebrush. Yet I've seen bull elk look right through bowhunters clad in ASAT 3D in the open sage and bull pine flats of New Mexico.

If you plan to hunt open terrain, give this unique camo pattern a try. I believe the combination of ASAT 3D, combined with a cow decoy, could be a real killing combination. I've noticed that other major camouflage manufacturers have also begun offering a 3D camo pattern, so whatever major brand name you prefer, you can now find a 3D pattern to suit your taste.

The No Mess Field Dressing method will take much of the toil out of the chore of removing your bull elk from the backcountry.

Chapter 10

No Mess Field Dressing

I was totally unprepared for my first elk kill. The extreme joy of seeing my first bull elk lying at my feet quickly faded when I discovered that I could not even budge the bull from where it lay wedged between two trees. My field dressing equipment consisted of a single blade pocket knife — a cheap one at that!

By the time I had field dressed and hung the elk meat, it was three hours later and I was so exhausted that I had to lie on the ground in a bloody heap until I could muster enough strength to begin packing the elk out. My bad experience soon grew worse. The tremendous weight of an elk hind quarter slung over my shoulder quickly exhausted me as I stumbled over that rough Idaho mountain. I literally had to take a nap after the first pack because all my strength had left me.

It's been many years since that first elk kill and my comedy of errors and ignorance field dressing it. Every year, I chuckle over the phone as sportsmen relate exhausting tales of mayhem during the field dressing chore. One guy from Wisconsin told me that he and his buddy were absolutely worn out after packing the first two quarters three miles over rugged terrain. They dreaded having to pack out the other two quarters plus the antlers and cape. He told me, "We got a pleasant surprise when we returned the next morning. A bear had drug the two quarters off into the brush. I hate to say it, but at the time, I wanted to kiss that bear's feet for helping us!"

The field dressing and packing chore is not a nightmare reserved for the newcomer to elk hunting, either. I know a lot of local hunters who just about bust a seam struggling with it. The good news is that there are ways to minimize the time and effort you have to put into the field dressing chore, and you won't lose an ounce of meat, either.

A couple of years ago, I was hunting with Jake Jones and his friend in a backcountry elk paradise in Oregon. Jake killed a dandy six-point bull one morning. He proudly showed me the huge bull and then moaned, "It's going to take us two packs to get this elk out of here."

I got both men's attention when I said, "We can pack everything out in one trip." I then proceeded to explain my method of no mess field dressing. Though Jake had killed five bulls with his bow, he had been field dressing and packing out his elk the hard way. I then showed the guys how I do it, and we each carried out just one hefty pack the five miles to the vehicles, much to the relief of Jake. All the way back to the vehicle, he kept mumbling, "I can't believe I packed all that useless stuff out with those other elk."

No Mess Field Dressing Is Born

The fourth bull that I killed with bow and arrow dropped in a real hell hole. It was three miles from the nearest road, in the bottom of a steep draw. Frankly, I was worried as I began opening up the bull's belly to remove the entrails. They say that necessity is the mother of invention, and I must agree with them when it comes to no mess field dressing.

Suddenly, a thought hit me. Why am I gutting this elk out? All the meat is on the outside of the ribcage, so why should I soak my entire body half-climbing into the ribcage? And as I thought about it a bit more, another idea hit me: Why pack out anything that isn't edible, such as bones?

Since that day, I have not gutted an elk, and I have not packed out a single bone. And I am proud to say that I have not wasted an ounce of edible meat, either. (Wasting meat is usually illegal.) The packing chore is still tough, but it's only a fraction of the toil it used to be.

No Mess Field Dressing

The first step with no mess field dressing is to wrestle the elk onto its back. Carefully open up the hide from the crotch up to the

Jake with his big Oregon bull. Jake learned from the author how to remove a big bull with a minimum of wasted meat and effort.

This hunter is removing the heavy leg bone from the elk quarters. All that will be packed out is the edible meat and ribs.

neck. Then begin peeling the hide from one side of the bull, starting at the belly and working the hide away from the carcass until you reach the backbone. After a while, you can allow the carcass to roll onto its unskinned side as you expose the front and rear quarters. Eventually, the carcass will be lying on its side with the unskinned side down, and you will have one entire side of the carcass exposed, with the skinned hide lying on the ground. Use this hide as a ground cover to place meat on as you butcher the carcass.

Next, carefully slice through the heavy meat on the rear ham where it meets the spine, until you have exposed the hip joint. Work the knife into that joint until the rear leg is severed from the hip socket. Lay that rear ham on the skinned hide and then remove the heavy leg bone. When you are done, you should have all the meat that was on that rear ham in one huge chunk, with no bone in it. Put that mass of meat into a game bag and put it aside because more meat will be going into that bag.

Next, remove the front shoulder. This is done by moving the front leg back and forth until you locate the shoulder blade. Work your knife between the underside of the shoulder blade and the

As huge as this bull may appear, there is only about 200 pounds of edible red meat to pack out if a hunter is smart and leaves behind the bones.

ribcage. The shoulder is not connected to the elk's body by any bones, so it comes off quick and easy. Lay the front shoulder on the hide and remove all the meat from the shoulder bone. Put that meat into the game bag with the other meat.

Next, carefully work your knife along that wonderful strip of filet meat that runs the length of the carcass along the spine and top of the ribcage. This is done by slicing along the spine on top, and then along the ribcage below. This meat will come off in a long strip. Put that meat into the game bag and then go back and slice off any small chunks of red meat that are still attached to the carcass when you removed the rear ham. While you're doing this, also remove as much neck meat as possible. These chunks of meat tend to be small, and are used mostly for grinding into burger.

When you're done, you'll have about 90 pounds of meat in one game bag. As you survey your work, you'll see that all the edible meat has been removed from one side of the carcass. Now it's just a simple chore to roll the elk over and repeat the process to remove all the edible meat from the other side of the carcass.

Eventually, you'll have two big bags of meat. The carcass

An elk's skull is very heavy and useless. Learn how to cape your elk head before taking your trip and avoid packing out this extra 35 pounds of bone.

will appear intact, except that all the edible meat has been removed. But you don't have to quit now. I love elk ribs, so I usually remove the rack of ribs from both sides of the carcass and also pack them out.

Once these ribs are removed, you can then carefully slip your knife under the spine on the inside of the carcass and remove the two tenderloins, which are found just before the hip joint.

Some folks also like the elk heart and liver, but you don't have to gut the entire carcass to retrieve them. Simply make a small incision where the liver and heart are located and remove them. Close the game bags and hang them in a tree in the shade to cool until you're ready to pack them out.

Now don't you see how a guy could totally field dress and hang a mature elk in an hour? If you consider the fact that bone counts for 60 percent of a gutted elk carcass, it's obvious that you've just saved yourself a lot of packing by leaving the bones behind.

Caping

There is no reason to panic if you want to save the elk's cape while no mess field dressing. Roll the bull on his back, and start the caping chore by ringing the chest with a hide incision that runs about six inches behind the front leg. Make another incision along the backbone and then work the hide over a shoulder and up the neck as far as possible. Forget about the caping chore at this point and proceed to peel the hide off the rear ham. Now remove the meat on that first side of the carcass.

When you turn the carcass on the other side, work the cape hide up to the neck on that side and then sever the head from the neck bone with a meat saw. Remove the rest of the meat using the no mess field dressing method.

An elk's head is a very heavy, useless mass of flesh and bone and it serves no good purpose to pack out this extra 35 pounds. Take a half hour and carefully peel the hide off the head. Caping a head is not exactly brain surgery. Anyone can do it, so be sure you learn how to cape a head before your hunt begins. (See Appendix A for appropriate books and videos on this subject.) Now simply saw off the antlers from the skinned head. While you're doing this, don't forget to remove the valuable ivory teeth from the elk's upper jaw.

The Packing Chore

The big problem with packing boned meat is a matter of logistics. You have these two heavy bags of meat, and the only way to pack one out after the boning job is to sling it over your shoulder. This is a good way to permanently ruin your shoulder and it is very dangerous to pack such a heavy load, precariously balanced on a shoulder, over rough forest terrain. Many serious back injuries have occurred from this foolhardy practice.

The only recourse, then, is to hike all the way back to camp or your vehicle to fetch a backpack. Then you have to hike all the way back to the hanging meat. You can see that a guy can get mighty tired even before the actual packing chore begins.

This happened so many times to me that I began carrying my backpack into the heart of the area where I intended to hunt and then stashing it. The problem was that I often roamed the mountains for miles in search of rutting bulls, and I sometimes killed a bull in a place where it would have been easier to hike back to camp. Instead, I often had to crawl way back up into some distant basin for no other

The collapsible pack frame can be assembled in a few minutes with no special tools and can save a lot of extra work for a hunter packing out an elk.

reason than to retrieve my stupid backpack!

The obvious answer was to keep the backpack with me, but backpacks are bulky and noisy, and no serious elk hunter could function effectively with one strapped on. I finally found a wonderful invention that has made this problem disappear forever. It is called a collapsible packframe. When broken down, this pack measures only 14 inches by four inches, weighs only three pounds, and can easily be carried in a backpack. It can be quickly assembled with no tools, and it can easily hold 90 pounds of meat.

No Mess Field Dress Gear

No mess field dressing will be made quicker and easier if you carry the proper field dressing utensils. My pack contains two large folding knives with two blades each, honed in advance to razor sharpness. Elk hair is very abrasive and quickly dulls cheap steel, so make sure you carry multiple sharp cutting blades of quality steel. A bone saw is also necessary for severing ribs, neck bones, and antlers.

Always carry a good supply of light nylon rope to tie the elk's legs apart while field dressing, hanging the game bags, and lashing the bags onto the packframe. Heavy duty elk game bags are needed for holding up to 90 pounds of elk meat. Very few sporting goods stores carry these types of bags in areas other than elk states. You might be wise to wait and purchase four of these bags when you arrive out West for your hunt, or order them from a catalog.

Overnight Gear

Yes, overnight gear and field dressing gear tend to go hand in hand. Several times, I've chosen to stay in the woods overnight rather than stumble out during the night carrying 100 pounds of meat. It's too easy to have an accident packing meat in the dark. My pack always contains enough provisions to take me comfortably through the night in the woods.

Overnight gear should include a small flashlight and extra batteries, Bic lighter to start a fire, lightweight food and water, plus an emergency shelter such as a large space blanket or small plastic tent. Also, carry orange plastic ribbon to flag your way in and out of the kill area. The thought of being alone out in the big woods overnight is mentally unsettling, but the reality is that a night spent in the woods close to your trophy is actually a very pleasurable and soothing experience.

However, I do want to give a word of caution here. If you hunt in grizzly bear country, make sure you camp at least a half mile away from your downed elk to avoid contact with any grizzly that might catch the scent of fresh blood overnight. And when you approach your kill next morning, make lots of noise and cautiously approach the carcass.

Conclusion

This entire field dressing business is no joke, and many hunters don't give enough thought or planning beforehand to how a huge bull elk they might kill will be removed from the backcountry.

Always pack overnight gear just in case you have to stay far back from camp overnight when field dressing an elk.

I get phone calls throughout the year from exuberant elk hunters who want to pack way back where the big bulls roam. When I ask how they intend to get an elk the five miles back to the trailhead, they tell me they're young and strong and very capable of packing an elk out. The difficult job, they tell me, is killing the elk. The rest just comes natural. Immediately, I know they've never killed and packed out an elk.

Chapter 11

Where All The Big Elk Live

I have never been a trophy hunter. The thrill of a close range encounter with a rutting bull elk has always been, and always will be, the epitome of a true trophy experience for me. How can a hunter complain when one of the most coveted big game animals in the world is standing broadside 20 yards away? In the state and national forests where I hunt in Idaho, Montana and Colorado, the average size bachelor bull will carry a five-point rack that would score about 230 points. This is a decent bull and nothing to be sneered at.

Still, there is a definite difference in the level of excitement when you hunt in an area where the average bachelor bull carries a six-point rack that would score about 300 points. I have had the privilege of hunting in a few trophy units in the past few years, and I have come to greatly appreciate the sport of hunting in areas that harbor lots of big bulls. Surprisingly, my reasons aren't solely for the sake of a record book trophy.

I love to hunt rutting bulls, and I greatly enjoy the drama and intensity of a natural rutting environment. But in many overhunted areas today, the natural rutting environment is missing. The pecking order of older mature herd bull (7 years), mature bachelor bull (5 years), and immature raghorn bull (3 years) has been eliminated. Instead, most public hunting areas now have herd bulls that are nothing more than immature four-points of 2 1/2 years of age.

In this environment, it is more difficult to hunt rutting bulls because the pecking order is missing. The angry, frustrated bachelor bull should be about five years old. Instead, he's two years old, and he can't figure out what the rut's about yet. This is one of the main reasons why so many hunters become confused and frustrated when calling at a bachelor bull that is just as confused about his status in the pecking order.

For that reason, I always seek out those backcountry areas where the natural pecking order is still intact among the elk. Unfortunately, these areas are becoming increasingly difficult to find and keep as the encroachment of civilization eliminates prime backcountry habitat. It's gotten to the point where you have to either purchase horses and pack several miles into a wilderness area, or plan to hunt in those areas that provide limited access.

The comparison between public and limited hunting was apparent in two hunts that I was on in Colorado and New Mexico. In Colorado, I hunted in a national forest area that held many elk. This hunting unit required a bull elk to be a four-point or better before it became legal game. However, Colorado's unlimited nonresident quota had brought tremendous pressure on the elk in this area. Consequently, most of the mature bulls had been shot off.

I hunted that area for seven days. During that time, I saw hundreds of elk, and many were bulls — all in the four-point class. The biggest bull I saw in seven days of hunting was a 5X6 herd bull. As strange as it sounds, I was able to "bugle" him away from his harem of cows. He came almost 200 yards to my position on a low ridge. I shot him as he stood broadside at 20 yards. He was a decent bull that would score about 240 points, but in the back of my mind, I wondered, "What kind of herd bull is this that would leave his cows and come in to my squeaky bugling?"

In contrast, I was the cameraman on a hunt in a New Mexico trophy area called the Valle Vidal. This is a limited entry unit. The elk herd is managed for trophy potential, which means only the surplus mature bulls are harvested by hunters. The natural order of a mature elk herd still exists in the Valle Vidal, and the action was fast and furious as frustrated mature bachelor bulls in the 300-330 range responded to our calling. It was pure joy to see a 300 point bull start coming in to our cow calling, then stop to run off a small five point bull who had the same idea, and then continue in to our cow calling.

The difference is obvious. When you hunt an area where the

In a natural herd environment, a bachelor bull may be a mature five year old animal with a rack in the 300 point range.

In areas of heavy hunting pressure, the bulls you'll find are usually immature animals.

natural elk herd exists, you not only have the opportunity to harvest a mature bull elk, but the rutting action is sure to be more intense and the bulls are more responsive to calling. The reason is simple. A five-year-old bachelor bull who is fully mature and half-insane with rutting lust is sure to be more aggressive and responsive to a radical challenge.

We can conclude that the best places to hunt rutting bulls are those places where the natural order among the bulls in the elk herd is still intact. Of course, that is pure Utopia in many areas of the West that currently are experiencing heavy hunting pressure. But even in states known for their inferior bull quality, such as Colorado, there are hunting units set aside solely for the purpose of trophy (meaning mature bulls) elk hunting.

My friend, Jim Zumbo, recently told me, "Hunters have no excuse for not hunting big bulls. My research has discovered that less than 10 percent of all elk hunters apply for trophy bull units. And many of these guys complain about the lack of quality bulls. I've also learned that 90 percent of the bulls taken in these trophy units are six-point or better. Statistics don't lie. Over 90 percent of the hunters are not even applying for those trophy units where a permit will virtually guarantee them a six-point bull."

Special hunt areas on public land are also valuable for the average hunter for one very important reason. While a trophy hunt on an exclusive private hunting area may run more than $10,000, one of these public area special permits usually only costs a couple hundred dollars to a nonresident, and usually far less for a resident.

I would strongly encourage any elk hunter who desires to experience the thrill of hunting for rutting bull elk in a natural herd situation to apply for any special hunts in his state. Unfortunately, the process of applying for trophy hunts in far away states where the application procedure is confusing, usually frustrates and discourages most aspiring trophy hunters.

The good news is that one western outfitter in particular has figured out a way to make these "big bull" trophy hunts accessible to the common man. George Taulman of U.S. Outfitters is by far the most successful and prolific elk outfitter in the country. George outfits more than 400 elk hunters alone throughout the West. I've been in his camps. They are not only top rate in accommodations, but he hires only the very best guides who have an intimate knowledge of elk and how to hunt them.

U.S. Outfitters now offers a licensing plan that is just too good for any serious elk hunter to pass up. Here's how it works: For a one-time fee of $100, George will enter your name in several drawings in several states for hunting units that offer limited access, trophy bull elk hunting. The hunt I filmed on the Valle Vidal trophy unit in New Mexico was a result of George's licensing program. George applied for the two Tennessee hunters and made sure their hunt was a success.

Here's the really unique part. U.S. Outfitters does not charge a $100 fee for each hunt it applies for you. That $100 fee is a one time charge. You may go a few years before you draw one of those coveted Arizona tags through George's licensing program, but the only fee you pay him is the one time $100 fee, which pays for his time and trouble in entering your name in the drawings. U.S. Outfitters has truly done both the common man and experienced trophy hunter a service by bringing true trophy hunts to the average sportsman.

Most hunters miss out on quality elk hunting areas because they do not apply for these limited entry units.

Where All The Big Bulls Live

The big bulls don't live where they're supposed to! A glance at the Boone & Crockett record book actually gives the reader a misleading notion that most of the big bulls are found in Montana. As I said before, statistics don't lie. Montana is credited with the most B&C bulls in the record book. However, if we dig deeper, we can see a trend in the past 15 years shifting this exalted status to the Southwest.

The reason why Montana has long been known as a top "big bull" trophy state is because, in the past, Montana had been an ideal elk state. It's semi-open terrain was excellent for nutritious grasses, and it's almost non-existent human population allowed the elk to not only eat good feed, but grow old. This combination, as I mentioned, is the best way to grow 375 point bulls. In the past 50 years, no other state could touch Montana for the production of Boone & Crockett bulls.

Unfortunately, that's all changed. Montana has been

The common man can still gain access to limited entry trophy elk hunting areas by applying for or allowing U.S. Outfitters to do it for them.

discovered — not just by a few rich movie stars, but also by a million other average American citizens who have become fed up with the frantic pace of urban life. They have come to the Big Sky state, and their presence has created intense hunting and habitat pressure on the elk.

I've seen this frustrating scenario unfold over the past 20 years. In places where I used to see huge old bulls, I now see raghorns. In roadless areas where the elk seldom encountered hunters, there are now easy access roads. For some strange reason, the folks who make policy in Montana have either not seen this as a problem or not identified it.

If you look at the record book for both the Boone & Crockett Club and the Pope & Young Club, you will notice a definite shifting to the Southwestern states of Arizona and New Mexico. There is good reason for this. After the Merriam elk was exterminated from Arizona in the 1930's, elk hunting virtually ceased. It wasn't until Yellowstone elk were privately transplanted into Arizona in 1940 that the elk herd began to grow. The story is essentially the same for New Mexico.

And grow they did! Though Arizona and New Mexico fall far short of big numbers for total elk populations, their trophy production cannot be denied. For instance, Colorado boasts a herd of 250,000 elk, while Arizona has only 12,000 elk in the entire state. But look at both record books, and you will see that both New Mexico and Arizona are the leaders in big bull entries. In fact, Arizona is the leading state for entries in the Boone & Crockett Club for the past 10 years, while New Mexico is by far the top state for Pope & Young Club entries. As I said, statistics don't lie, and they are telling us that the big bull production has shifted to those states where quality has taken precedence over quantity.

Every spring, the Montana Department of Fish, Wildlife, & Parks holds local sportsmen's meetings where they solicit comments from individuals. I stand up every spring and request more quality bull elk hunting be cultivated. I usually get shouted down by the good old boy crowd who want to go out and shoot a spike for meat.

In contrast, New Mexico and Arizona don't have the big elk herds, so sportsmen are not prone to want to kill every elk just because it's an elk. There just aren't enough elk for everyone to kill.

If you check the record books, you will notice a definite shifting of trophy entries in the past decade to Southwest states.

The good news is that more state wildlife agencies are setting aside overhunted areas for quality bull elk hunting.

As a result, limited entry is allowed in most hunting units. This translates to a controlled number of hunters being allowed to enter a certain hunting unit. These hunters take only a few of the bulls, and since they are not in severe competition with each other, these hunters tend to hold back and take only the very best bulls, often passing up mature six-point bulls that "only" score about 300 points.

Today, the big bulls live in the Southwestern states of New Mexico and Arizona. However, Utah and Nevada are also gaining big bull areas as their elk herds continue to grow and wildlife officials carefully control the harvest. In the meantime, the big meat-hunter states of Oregon, Washington, Colorado, Montana and Idaho continue to allow spike bulls to be harvested, with the result being a juvenile elk herd.

Fortunately, there is some good news on the horizon for these meat-hunting states. New controlled-hunt opportunities are appearing in areas where the mature bull elk have been shot out. State wildlife biologists, out of professional pride or as the result of browbeating by a disgusted public, have begun to manage more and more prime elk units for trophy management.

I also firmly believe that education from conservation groups, such as the Rocky Mountain Elk Foundation, has greatly helped the average sportsman understand the value of the elk herd as a precious resource that continues to get better and better if it is managed more as a resource than as a source of winter meat. Where do all the big elk live? They can live just about anywhere from the high country parks of the Montana wilderness to the deserts of Nevada. All they need is a chance to grow.

Alternative Elk Hunting Areas

The process of obtaining a tag for a limited entry area can sometimes be too slow for certain sportsmen. It often takes years to get drawn for some of the more coveted trophy elk hunting units, so many sportsmen have discovered private ranches as a great source of natural herd elk hunting.

Paul Brunner and I discussed this issue a few weeks ago. He told me, "I swore I'd never pay to go elk hunting, but things are getting so bad on public ground that I have decided to pay money to a landowner for the privilege of hunting a natural elk herd."

There are many large cattle raising companies which now allow natural herd elk hunting for a nominal fee, while other private landowners offer guided and semi-guided hunts.

Paul added, "Last year in the Centennial Mountains of Montana, I had hunters cut right in front of me as I was working a bull in. What amazed me was that these guys knew exactly what they were doing. They just shrugged their shoulders and laughed when I told them in no uncertain terms that I felt they were not very sporting. That experience was enough for me. I've started applying for limited entry hunts. In the meantime, I'm willing to pay to hunt private land."

There are many large cattle companies across the West. Their main business is cattle ranching, which is done in the lower bottom lands. However, huge herds of elk roam the more rugged arroyos and ridges. These cattle companies charge a flat fee for access to hunt these prime elk areas. Other cattle companies have begun their own outfitting business as a sideline to the cattle business.

Let me make one thing very clear. These are not tame elk! They are as wild and cautious as any elk on public land. They're just not hunted hard, so the natural pecking order is intact, and a bugling hunter usually gets plenty of action with big bulls.

Several Native American tribes have also entered into the trophy elk hunting business. Tribes such as the Mescalero and Jacarilla, and the White Mountain Apache have come to symbolize quality elk hunting. U.S. Outfitters also offers exclusive private land hunts. You can find the addresses of these outfitters in Appendix B.

Even though our elk herds are generally healthy today, there are some negative forces that could have far ranging consequences for elk hunting.

Chapter 12

Positive And Negative Influences on The Elk Herd

Elk are very large, powerfully built animals that inhabit mostly backcountry. Yet for all their impressive size and preference for isolation, elk are very susceptible to the whims of mankind.

You need only look at the historic distribution of elk to see just how much impact civilization has had on the elk of North America. Archaeologists have discovered remains of elk in every state in the continental United States, and elk were frequently seen by the Pilgrims along the East Coast.

The encroachment of civilization literally wiped the elk off the face of the earth in a matter of 100 years, except for those few rugged mountain areas in the West that were too isolated and rough for hide hunters to bother with. That, literally, is where our present day elk herd came from.

Even though the overall conservation effort of the elk from the dismal days of 1900 to the present is truly a success story, there are forces today that still have a tremendous impact on the elk herd. Some of these forces are positive, and some are negative. And interestingly enough, some of those impact forces that have always been considered negative, are actually slowly turning positive, while other more favorably viewed forces may have a very negative impact on the elk herd.

Positive Influences

The absolutely most positive influence on today's elk herd comes from the Rocky Mountain Elk Foundation. The RMEF

A truly historic agreement was recently signed by major timber companies, the U.S. Forest Service and the Rocky Mountain Elk Foundation to include elk management in any land decisions.

membership totals over 100,000. Obviously, this is a strong organization, but there are other sporting fraternities with far greater memberships, such as Ducks Unlimited and The Wild Turkey Federation.

What sets the RMEF apart is their dedication to the acquisition of elk habitat, whether through purchase, easements, leasing, or habitat agreements. These folks can find just about any way there is to provide a haven for elk. And we all know that without proper habitat, the elk herd simply would not exist as it is today.

Here's a good example of one of the unique, no astounding, ways the RMEF has devised to preserve and manage elk habitat. Last week, I was sent to video the signing of some sort of historic conservation agreement at the RMEF headquarters in Missoula, Montana. It wasn't until the meeting began, and I was running the camera, that the true impact of the enormous historical importance of that meeting struck me. And let me tell you, it hit me like a ton of bricks!

You see, I've known that the RMEF has worked hard to provide and improve elk habitat, but many of their efforts were frustrated because other landowners were managing their land contrary to sound elk conservation procedures.

An example of this was the U.S. Forest Service practice of logging. Even though one of the basic principles of the Forest Service is supposed to be wildlife management on their lands, it is a sad fact that most of the federal land was managed for logging. Elk can tolerate some logging activity, but full scale commercial logging has had a very detrimental effect in these areas that were over-logged.

However, through the efforts of the RMEF, the Forest Service has agreed to accommodate the special needs of the elk in any management plans. Unfortunately, there were other very large landowners in the West who threatened to ruin any conservation practice begun by the RMEF and the Forest Service.

Forest Service land that was nurtured for elk habitat was virtually negated by large timberland owners such as Weyerhauser, Potlatch and Plum Creek. These companies would totally strip their land that adjoined a special federal land tract managed for elk, and the result would be devastating. Access roads would be pushed right up to the federal land, valuable cover was stripped off, and the elk usually disappeared from that area. It was very frustrating to see this scenario played out time and time again.

One thing I want to make perfectly clear is that this is not an indictment of the big timber companies. We live in America where the mode of life revolves around the free enterprise system, and these large companies are run to make a profit. They have every right to do whatever it takes to turn a profit. The problem is that these large timber companies own hundreds of millions of acres of prime elk habit on which their trees grow.

Some farsighted folks at the RMEF were able to convince these large timber companies that it would be in their best interest to manage their lands for both timber and wildlife. They were convinced that both could be accommodated at no extra cost to the private companies, and the publicity would finally put these much-maligned private timber companies in a more favorable light.

So it was that I videoed this historical signing of a

Elk need seclusion. They won't tolerate the encroachment of civilization like a whitetail deer.

conservation agreement between the RMEF, U.S. Forest Service, and several mega-large private timber landowners. These folks were far removed in their everyday work practices, but they came together that day to pledge support for the protection of critical elk habitat.

This agreement states that when a particular area of land is identified as essential for the existence of the resident elk herd, that land, often totaling thousands of acres, would be managed to retain its quality as elk habitat — no matter whether it is on federal or Weyerhauser land. That, folks, is akin to having a peace agreement signed by the United States, Russia, Iran, Iraq and China!

Another positive influence on the elk herd is the growing practice by state wildlife officials to set aside prime elk units for limited entry hunting of trophy size bulls. This practice may appear to some to be nothing more than an elitist practice for "big-head" hunters, but in fact its main goal is to manage the elk at a near natural herd level.

The non-hunting public views folks who hunt these areas as true sportsmen who are willing to pass over most of the elk and take only those few surplus bulls who are not essential to the maintenance of the herd. Compare that to the adverse publicity that a juvenile elk herd gives to sportsmen. Non-hunters hear about herds that contain only four mature bulls per 100 cows, and you can see how the average person on the street, when asked for their opinion about hunting, would condemn it.

Negative Influences

The encroachment of civilization on prime habitat is by far the most negative influence on the elk herd. Elk are not like deer. They can't just move over a bit to accommodate housing developments and ski resorts. A friend of mine back in Pennsylvania purchased a new home five years ago in an exclusive secluded subdivision. The land developer had purchased an isolated hardwood ridge which contained about 1,000 acres. The beautiful old oak trees were removed, and all other brush and trees were bulldozed into piles and burned. At the time the development began, that area held about 100 whitetail deer.

Five years later, 400 houses now sit where oak forest once stood. How are the poor deer faring? Quite well, thank you! The current population is about 650 deer. Instead of running away, the whitetail deer, as it has always done, has simply adapted. Deer now roam backyards and dine on tasty garden vegetables, flowers and expensive rhododendrons. It's gotten so bad that the folks in that subdivision, largely non-hunters and anti-hunters, had to get together and do something about the deer plague. You guessed it! They created their own private special hunting season, and archers can be seen in treestands harvesting deer just 100 yards from half million dollar homes.

Elk aren't like that. They need seclusion. They won't tolerate the encroachment of civilization nearly as much as the very adaptable whitetail deer. Subdivisions in the West usually pop up in lowland, gentle sloping areas which are normally winter range for the elk. These areas are critical for elk to exist. When the mountains are buried under deep snow, the elk need these lowland areas where snow remains low and the grass greens up early in spring. When homes take over these wintering areas, the elk population suffers and dwindles.

Western states need to have their professional land planners study any proposed subdivision for more than the usual things such as sewer, water and visual impact. They must also decide whether the resident wildlife, such as elk and mule deer, will be adversely affected by the construction of 100 houses in a place where these animals normally winter.

Meat hunting is another very negative influence, for more reasons than one. Wholesale slaughter of an elk herd to the point where bulls are not allowed to grow to maturity creates a biological imbalance. Every state that allows unlimited elk hunting by residents is now experiencing a severe shortage of mature bulls in most public hunting areas. Only those few backcountry areas where access is by horse remain in a natural herd condition.

This is not only a poor biological practice, it also has a tremendously adverse impact on the sport of hunting. Ultimately, public opinion will dictate whether hunting will continue as a valid form of recreational herd management. As we all know, public support of hunting has been dwindling at an alarming rate. Today, the majority of non-hunters would vote against hunting. And the more they hear about the wholesale slaughter of immature elk, the lower their opinion becomes of hunting as a form of game

Every state that now allows unlimited hunting is experiencing a shortage of mature bull elk.

management.

I truly love the sport of elk hunting. However, I am willing to give up a year of hunting for elk every now and then to insure that the elk herd is maintained at a natural level. Oh, come on. You can take a year off from elk hunting once in a while! You can take that dream hunt for caribou, or go after that big muley buck you never seem to have time for! Folks, the state of the western elk herds is getting to that stage where we sportsmen must go to our wildlife agencies and offer these types of concessions, or else some federal judge will do it for us as a result of a lawsuit by an animal rights group.

Surprisingly, one of the greatest dangers to the future of elk and elk hunting in the Rockies may come, in my opinion, from the reintroduction of the wolf. Already, there have been fierce court battles between pro wolf and anti wolf factions, and the pro wolf folks have won out. Many wolves have already been reintroduced into Idaho, Montana and Wyoming.

On the surface, this seems like sound wildlife management. The wolf is simply being reintroduced to its historic range. However, there is an underlying agenda and plan by the animal rights, anti-hunting faction to turn the wolf into the ultimate wildlife pawn.

As we sportsmen have already painfully discovered, one decision by a federal judge in San Francisco can have a devastating affect on wildlife in the Montana wilderness, as it did with our grizzly bear hunting season. And since the wolf reintroduction has already been mandated by a federal court, it would seem logical for that same federal court to insure the welfare of the wolf. So when the wolf population grows large enough to begin competing with sportsmen for food in the form of game, who do you think the

The reintroduction of the federally protected gray wolf into western game ranges may bring about a confrontation between hunters and wolf management policy.

federal court will side with?

I greatly fear that some federal judge, when faced with the question of allowing elk to be taken by hunters or wolves, will choose the latter. That decision could have the potential to eliminate huge tracts of federal land as a hunting ground for the wolf. This reasoning may seem far fetched to you, but as a trapper, I've been fighting the cunning moves of the animal rights faction long before the average hunter was even aware of the threat. Please pay special attention to the wolf issue, even though you may live a long distance from the controversy.

And please don't misinterpret my wolf comments. I am not anti-wolf. I love wolves, and I have made a hobby of documenting wolf sightings over the past 20 years. However, I do believe we should all be aware that the animal rights, anti-hunting faction could use the wolf to try to stop elk hunting. We must be vigilant and make sure that any wildlife decisions concerning elk are made for the benefit of the elk, and not its predators.

This Colorado bull is proof that careful management of elk herds can produce both quantity and quality. Photo courtesy of Eagle Spirit Outfitters.

Chapter 13

Where Is Elk Hunting Headed?

There is a definite trend in elk hunting toward those areas where the elk are not subjected to heavy hunting pressure. Many seasoned hunters that I know who had always been adamant about keeping their elk hunting pure and free of commercialization — now are grudgingly switching to some form of limited entry hunting, whether it is in a state-sponsored drawing or on private land where access is gained at a price.

As I've mentioned, this is not a veiled form of elitism. Instead, it is born from the serious elk hunter's burning desire to encounter the rutting bull elk in a natural elk environment where mature herd bulls still rule the woods. I'm not a trophy hunter, but I also yearn for that pristine setting free from undue human pressure.

Many western states have recognized this need and set aside special hunting units for the hunter who wants to meet the bull elk in a natural herd setting. Consequently, there are many trophy hunting areas in just about all the western states where a sportsman eventually will draw a limited entry permit. That's the good news.

The bad news is that many of these same enterprises who have created natural herd hunting have also created a monster in the form of elitism due to extreme fees. For example, New Mexico's famed Valle Vidal trophy elk hunting unit is the epitome of a trophy elk unit. Mature herd bulls seven years old roam the pristine high country meadows or pine flats, and bachelor bulls tend to be mature

There is a definite trend in elk hunting toward those areas where elk are not subjected to heavy hunting pressure.

six-pointers scoring in the low 300's. It is a wonderful place to hunt, and of course, entry is by permit only.

Unfortunately, that state's wildlife officials have decided that anyone who might want to hunt trophy bull elk must be rich, so they have tripled the permit fee from $300 to $850. Such special permit gouging is sure to create a situation where only the most affluent of sportsmen can afford this famed hunting unit. Unfortunately, I'm not one of them. I had planned to apply for the Valle Vidal, but that huge price increase has left me stunned, bewildered — and a bit angry at the price gouging by some western states to cash in on the honest desire by the common man to pursue the bull elk in a natural herd setting.

For the hunter who just wants to hunt bull elk, trophy or not, there is lots of good news. Some states, such as Colorado, have been able to manage their elk herd to accommodate both heavy hunting pressure and quality. Colorado has done this by allowing unlimited nonresident access to that state, but allowing only branch antlered bulls to be hunted in many areas. Colorado has been knocked for

This dandy bull was taken on the Mescalero Indian Reservation, which manages its lands for trophy elk hunting.

allowing too many hunters in the field to kill too many of the mature bulls, but for many hunters, the opportunity to kill a four-point bull elk is the fulfillment of a lifetime dream.

Montana and Idaho also try hard to accommodate as many resident and nonresident hunters as they feel the elk herd can endure. Both of these states have first-come, first-served nonresident license sales and both have quotas, but it is not too difficult to get a license if you are prompt with your application. In addition, Montana has begun providing unlimited nonresident elk tags for outfitters, but these special outfitter elk tags are expensive — about $800. However, most outfitters are willing to pay this added expense to gain the nonresident client's business.

So you see, there is reason for optimism for both the trophy elk hunter and the common guy who just wants to enjoy the excitement of the elk hunt. There is cause for even more optimism as more elk transplants, into areas not known for elk hunting, are experiencing unprecedented success. The Rocky Mountain Elk Foundation has been responsible for numerous elk transplants into

Midwest, Southwest, and even Eastern states. A few uninformed hunters have scoffed at this practice as creating an unnatural elk herd in non-elk habitat.

At one time, various species of elk inhabited almost all of North America. Elk bones and Native American art have proven beyond a shadow of a doubt that elk roamed the eastern hardwoods when the Pilgrims first set foot on American soil. Elk were numerous in the upper midwestern states, and elk bones have even been found as far south as Louisiana. Consequently, a thriving elk herd that allows limited elk hunting in Wisconsin is not an aberration, but is biologically accurate. Limited hunting has already begun in a few of these areas where the elk herd has grown beyond the land's carrying capacity. Wouldn't it be great fun to see a big bull come stomping forward through the Wisconsin birch trees in response to your bugling?

Probably the most serious threats to elk hunting come from two sources. One is obvious, while the other is much more subtle, but with frightening potential.

Adverse Public Opinion

The American public, as I have mentioned, will ultimately decide the fate of elk hunting. If we sportsmen can portray hunting and hunters as true sportsmen who care deeply about the land and the animals we hunt — then we should have no problems. Unfortunately, Americans throughout the country were shown just the opposite this past year as two major investigative news programs featured the greed and hypocrisy of a few elk poachers.

I speak specifically of the infamous Don Lewis affair. Don was an up and coming hunting personality whose tremendous trophy totals had already won him sponsorship, meaning money, from several major archery manufacturers. In return for the money, Don would testify that he would rather quit hunting than take to the field without Brand X. What a crock!

This demeaning of sportsmen with the type of manufacturer's hype such as you see in magazines today is exactly the opposite of what archery hunting needs. When some guy appears with his ugly mug in a full page color photo in a major outdoor magazine, stating, "When I want results, I use only the best — Brand X!" Of course, he

This photo showing Don Lewis with one of his illegal elk kills was pulled off the video film that appeared on televisions all over the country.

doesn't bother to add that Brand X is not any better than any of the other similar products out there, or that he was paid hundreds, or even thousands, of dollars to be associated with that product.

Folks, there is almost no difference in major brands of bows and arrows. And all the bells and whistles that these "sudden experts" pitch at us sportsmen through unabashed advertising should be discouraged by responsible sportsmen through letters-to-the-editor, or letters to major manufacturers. As long as these manufacturers believe that the average hunter is gullible enough to believe this advertising hype, we can expect a certain element of hunters with blind ambition who are willing to go to unbelievable extremes to be considered one of these "experts."

That, unfortunately, was the situation with Don Lewis. I'd met Don at a sporting show previously, and I truly liked the man. Don's trophy photo album was astonishing. Monster muley and whitetail bucks and near-world-record size bull elk filled the album. Yet even as I viewed those photos, I felt a pang of suspicion. As an experienced hunter, I knew that there were only a few of those really big bucks and bulls out there, and a dedicated sportsman might be able to harvest one or two of these top trophy animals in a lifetime — but this guy was killing a half dozen each year!

Don Lewis had already landed several lucrative promotional contracts when fate intervened. A game warden in Utah's famed Paunsaugant mule deer trophy area stopped a pickup truck and found a mule deer head and cape in the back. The deer season had ended, so the warden checked the deer. The owner, a Mr. Don Lewis of Alabama, told the warden he'd legally killed the muley in Arizona and had stopped at the Paunsaugant only to take pictures. The warden was suspicious, but since the deer had been legally tagged, he had to allow Lewis to continue on.

However, a few hours later, the warden met a photographer who reported finding a freshly poached, headless deer carcass in the area where the warden had stopped Lewis. Eventually, Lewis was cornered near Kanab, Utah with several fresh mule deer heads and capes. During the inspection of Lewis' pickup, state officials found a videotape, which was confiscated.

Eventually, someone stuck the tape into a VCR and it revealed several archery elk kills by Lewis and another man. The bulls were enormous! This caused suspicion among investigators, plus the fact that some of the terrain shown on the video had recently burned. On a whim, the tape was sent to officials at Yellowstone National Park.

The reaction at Yellowstone was akin to the eruption of Old Faithful geyser! Officials there immediately identified several prominent mountains on the videotape and an investigation began immediately. Lewis and another man would eventually plead guilty to poaching elk in Yellowstone National Park.

Though this truly was a sordid affair, it appeared on the surface no different from a handful of elk poachings that occur in our National Parks annually. But this one was different, because it carried ramifications far beyond the poaching charges.

Somehow, the major news networks picked up on the case and two investigative news programs featured Lewis and his illegal activities on their national broadcasts. The public was shown two bowhunters giggling, bragging, wounding and killing protected bull elk in our nation's greatest park. It was a tremendous black eye for sport hunting in general — and archery hunting in particular.

There is nothing we sportsmen can do to undo the harm done by this incident, other than to patiently explain that true sportsmen are the exact opposite of what was seen on the Lewis tape. However, there is something we can do to discourage future repetitions.

You must understand that Don Lewis killed and wounded those bulls out of blind ambition. He wanted to be famous and make money. In other words, if Lewis had not been caught, many elk hunters would be gladly paying $20 today to listen to Don Lewis speak at a seminar at some big sporting show, and they'd sit on the end of their seats sucking in every word, taking notes, and marveling at the sight of a super elk hunter. And they'd pay hundreds of dollars to purchase the exact brand of bow, arrows, broadheads, quiver, toilet paper, etc., etc., that Lewis was plugging.

It is this adverse publicity caused by infamous incidents, such as the Lewis affair and other more recent sordid incidents, which the general public is reading about and watching on television. Is it any wonder, then, that public opinion is shifting away from sport hunting? We need to counter this trend by joining true conservation

Public opinion toward hunting will ultimately decide the fate of our cherished sport.

Game farms allow a person to kill a big bull elk without expending any time and effort, but they send the wrong message to the public about sport hunting.

organizations, such as the Rocky Mountain Elk Foundation, and strongly voicing our objections when some "instant hero" comes forward hocking a product for money and making outlandish performance claims.

Game Farms & Elk Farms

I was visiting an outfitter friend in eastern Montana a few years ago during hunting season, and on one particular evening he brought two distinguished gentlemen back to the lodge. The men had just flown in from New York City. They were wealthy, important men, I was told. They were dressed from head to toe in brand new, expensive hunting clothes. They showed me their firearms. They were Weatherby 300 magnums, inlaid in gold and silver. They were beautiful guns, but I eventually cornered my outfitter friend and mentioned that those new guns were going to get a few scratches put on them, because the terrain was rugged and rocky.

My outfitter friend said, "Oh, these guys won't be hunting on my place. I'm taking them over to a game farm to hunt elk." I was astounded! A game farm? How could he? He replied that some guys don't have the time or desire to hunt hard for elk, so the local game farm does a service for these busy executives who want to enjoy the thrill of the hunt and quickly kill something, so they can get back to work — all within a few days.

Those two men departed the next morning after a leisurely breakfast and returned the next day with three bull elk racks — nothing more. How, I asked, did they end up with three racks? My outfitter friend sadly shook his head and related the story.

It seems the two men were so inept at hunting and moving through the woods that they had difficulty killing even a game farm bull in the 20 acre penned enclosure. Eventually, one of the men shot a bull, but the other guy just couldn't get the job done, so they had to stay overnight.

The next morning, the elk were at their feeding station, so the hunter had an easy 50 yard shot at a bull broadside. He did a good job. In fact, he did the job too good! The bullet tore through the chest of the bull he was shooting at, but then continued on and mortally wounded another bull that had been standing behind the first bull. The man was charged $6,000.00 for each bull he killed. And

Extremely tight elk farm regulations are necessary to avoid domestic diseases and red deer interbreeding in the wild elk herd.

here's the kicker. He was really proud of the fact that he'd killed two bull elk with a single shot. Wow! What a man!

I was a guest at that lodge, so I quickly departed for the woods to avoid an ugly scene and I stayed away for a long time until the men had left with their "trophies" for the airport. I would imagine their employees sat on the edge of their seats listening to stories of superhuman feats of determination and endurance by these two men who had flown from New York City to the wilds of Montana and brought back three trophy bull elk to prove their manhood — all in just three days.

Contrary to what you may have heard, game farm elk hunting is growing as more and more wealthy men are willing to pay to bring home a big elk rack. It is a disturbing trend that, if you think about it, fits in only too well with CD-ROM hunting games, the Internet, and our growing penchant to gain satisfaction the quickest and easiest way possible. And for some people, it's a bull elk shot standing at a feeding trough in a pen.

And the really frightening thing about it is that I don't know what can be done to dissuade men from killing elk the easy way just because they can afford it. I wish I could climb up on my self-righteous soap box and lecture sportsmen of the dangers of elk game farm hunting, but the sad fact of the matter is that everyone is free to do whatever they want to do, within the limits of the law. And currently, elk game farm hunting is legal and viewed by the states as a commercial venture. But to the general public (Remember them — the ones who will ultimately decide the fate of sport hunting?), game farm hunting only serves to solidify their mistaken opinion that all elk hunters are out there for the sole purpose of bringing back an ego-satiating rack of antlers.

Elk farms have the potential for far ranging damage to the elk herd. In western Montana, elk harvested near an exotic elk farm where red deer had escaped, were found to carry red deer genes. Obviously, interbreeding had begun and threatens to spread these foreign genes throughout the elk herd. The danger here is that the pure strain of elk in America may be adulterated as more and more of these red deer escape and interbreed with American elk. Currently, the danger is minimal, but this is an area of concern of wildlife officials in western states and should be monitored to insure our elk herds stay free of contamination from red deer.

Just as disturbing is more recent news from Canada that an elk in a game farm had developed mad cow disease. This disease, if it should enter into the wild elk herd, could devastate our herds. These are reasons why state wildlife officials often appear to be overly strict and heavy handed with private citizens who want to raise elk in captivity. They have identified these areas of danger to our wild elk herd and are adamant about stringent controls on any commercialization of wild animals. You can greatly help these officials by publicly voicing your support for extremely tight controls on all game farms and elk farms. If disease and interbreeding should run rampant in our elk herds, the question of sport hunting may become a moot point.

In conclusion, we can definitely see some bright spots in the future of elk hunting. More intense management of elk and their habitat is sure to provide optimum hunting conditions for sportsmen for years to come. However, we must also recognize that the elk is not an inexhaustible resource. Besides the game farm/elk farm problem, there are only so many elk, and the number of hunters desiring to pursue them increases annually. Therefore, it is imperative that we do everything within our power to provide suitable habitat for elk in order to insure the future of elk hunting for our children. You can do your part by joining The Rocky Mountain Elk Foundation, 2291 W. Broadway, Missoula, MT 59802-1813 (1-800-CALL-ELK).

My desire is to get so close to an elk that I can almost touch it.

Chapter 14

To Touch An Elk

The sun peeked over the horizon, spraying a sudden ray of amber light across the frost-covered mountain maple I crouched behind. My breath came in ragged gasps. Beads of perspiration trickled down my face and my entire body trembled. Suddenly the bushes exploded in a shower of leaves and twigs.

I jerked my head up and caught sight of a long, sweeping antler. Less than 10 feet away, a huge, rut-crazed bull elk was doing his best to destroy the bush — his disposition being nothing short of enraged. And I had a lot to do with it. He trotted toward my concealed position, bellowing out rage and frustration, then dropped his mighty rack and rammed into the bush. Dirt sprayed through the brush as his powerful legs churned the forest floor. My breath now came in quick, convulsive spurts.

Pieces of leg and neck and antlers flashed through the screen of leaves and limbs as I slowly raised my bow, preparing for that deadly, bittersweet moment. I sucked in a deep breath and dropped my mouth to the grunt tube slung over my shoulder. Bugling a challenge, I quickly brought my fingers up to the bowstring.

The mayhem on the other side of the bush suddenly stopped. A few seconds later a hollow, guttural growl sent a reflexive shiver up my spine. The elk's huge head appeared first, a glaring eyeball scanned for the intruder. A beautiful sweep of antlers followed, with his chest coming into view a second later. Only four paces away, he turned to stare at the strange form beside him. By the time his eyes began to register alarm, my arrow zipped forward and buried deep in his chest just behind the shoulder. The bull grunted, spun around, and smashed through the wall of brush. A few seconds later there was an enormous crash, followed by silence. The bull was down.

Great waves of emotion swept through me as I ran my hands over the hugh body, the chocolate-brown main beams and tips polished to an ivory shine. As they gradually subsided, a strong sense of satisfaction remained. I was grateful and gratified that a single well-placed arrow traveled just four yards. That's the way I want it — as close as I can get.

The gush of adrenalin and the awesome sight of a bull elk, almost close enough to touch, only fuels my desire to get closer. The perfect hunting scenario for me is a bellowing, rut-fevered bull-elk coming within five yards, lustfully tearing up the brush that stands between us, only to suddenly wind me, leaving me with a lingering sense of awe over being so close to such a powerful animal.

I wasn't always like this. Back in Pennsylvania, I had a "normal" attitude toward bowhunting. I had killed nearly two dozen whitetails with a bow, so considered myself an accomplished archer. Although I had no knowledge of the world of elk, I'd reasoned, "Wasn't an elk just a big deer?"

I read everything I could find on hunting elk with a bow and arrow, but at that time there was very little in print. About the only thing I had gleaned was that bull elk would come blissfully out of hiding if you tooted just right on a length of plastic pipe. So one crisp September morning, with an ignorance nearly as pristine as the lonely ridge in northern Idaho where I sat, I emitted a shrill call.

What happened next electrified me so completely that I've not been the same since. A haunting hollow squeal like the cry of a wilderness ghost floated through the high-country air, raising the hair on the back of my neck. In my excitement to bugle again, I blew too hard on the tube and the wooden plug flew out the other end, producing a noise closer to the dying throes of a vacuum cleaner than a bull elk's bugle.

It didn't matter. Another bugle came back at me almost immediately, but this time much closer. I stepped behind a small fir tree, searching the terrain over my shoulder just in case the bull might timidly slip in from behind. Then I bugled again. That bull came forward with all the timidity of a runaway freight train. Heavy

My first encounter with a rutting bull elk electrified me.

hooves pounded on the forest floor, branches snapped and suddenly an enormous bull elk burst out of a small thicket not more than 40 yards away.

I cowered behind the fir, hoping he wouldn't see me. My immediate desire was self-preservation. About the time I spied a nearby tree to climb, the bull got side-tracked. Twenty yards from my violently shaking body, he lunged into a small fir tree. I watched transfixed as he grunted, throwing his powerful body against the poor sapling with abandon.

It must have been the prehistoric hunter within me who nocked the arrow. Half dazed, I stepped out, drew back and released. The bull charged out of sight. But I noticed that he stumbled just before disappearing into the trees.

A short time later, I dropped to my knees in shock beside the huge bull. The arrow had done its job quickly, and the bull had run only 80 yards before going down. That first bull elk hooked me forever on the thrill of close-range elk hunting. My entire being yearned for the next bull elk to break cover and trot forward.

But a few years later, while working as a timber faller, a

Over the years, I've killed about a dozen bulls with a compound bow.

The love I have for these magnificent creatures pulls me to get as close to them as possible.

serious accident cast a long shadow across my future as a bowhunter. Surgery repaired the damage to my right shoulder, but I could hardly pull my recurve to full-draw, much less hold it there. Reluctantly, I tried out a compound bow — and found that the letoff enabled me to shoot. At the target range, I was amazed at its accuracy.

Over the years I killed close to a dozen elk with the compound bow, aluminum arrows and pre-sharpened broadheads. But during all this time, something was missing. The magic that first swept over me on that ridge in Idaho had gone out of the hunt and left me feeling like an observer — more a technician than a natural hunter. I realized I was missing what for me is the very core of bowhunting rutting elk.

I knew I could get into close-range encounters using either compound or recurve — that was up to me — but the recurve bow demanded it. I hungered for the familiarity of my recurve and the frantic action at "touching" range. I missed the pungent smell of cedar arrows, the soft feel of turkey feathers and the methodical sharpening of each broadhead to a razor's edge. But most of all, I missed the intimacy of pulling back the bow and shooting with pure instinct — the feeling that it was me who was solely responsible for sending that deadly shaft to its mark.

Slowly, I began exercising my shoulder, lifting weights and doing pushups. Six months later, I began gingerly shooting my recurve again. Now, after years of regular practice, I'm extremely confident of my accuracy out to 20 yards. But at 30 yards, well, you wouldn't want to be the guy with the apple on his head.

That's fine with me. I took up the bow long ago with the express purpose of challenging myself to hunt well enough to get almost within touching distance of my quarry. The reason I bowhunt, what draws me like a magnet, is that feeling of oneness with the wild animals I hunt — not as an intruder, but as a vital part of nature. I remember especially those unique moments when I have been present, undetected, within an arm's reach of elk. Like the morning a calf elk stood no more than five feet away calling for its mother. Or the afternoon I set up for a herd bull, only to turn around and find myself eyeball to eyeball with a young bull who'd slipped up behind me like a big cat. Or the time when a satellite bull charged into the thicket I was calling from — and literally knocked me backwards.

Suddenly, the bull is there.

The love I have for these magnificent creatures pulls me to get as close to them as possible. So I roam the breathtaking, lonely high country, calling and listening, hoping and waiting for a reply. When it comes, echoing off nearby canyon walls, the once-important issues of "Who am I" and "What am I" dissolve into a simple yearning to get close to the unseen bull that answered my call.

I slip forward and bugle again. The bull hammers back almost immediately. I feverishly scan the terrain and decide that he will come through a low swale between two ridges. I bugle once more and the monarch answers, no more than 60 yards ahead. I charge forward, risking detection, then kneel at the edge of a small stand of spruce saplings.

Gently, I place the palm of my right hand on the soft forest floor. My primal sense takes over, and I feel and listen for the bull. Suddenly, I "feel" the vibrations of oncoming hoofbeats, and a white hot surge of adrenalin scorches through my body.

The involuntary trembling begins, and my mind is suddenly free of everything else but the awareness that just out of sight is a huge surly beast — and he's looking for me.

Branches snap and heavy hoofbeats now reward my straining ears, and I gulp in huge gasps of air. My bow is up, and my concentration is keen, for I know what comes next. It is that bittersweet moment of death.

An antler tip emerges above the saplings not more than 15 steps away and floats forward. A branch snaps, then another. The swish of hair against brush, and antlers scraping against limbs, cause my shooting hand to grip the string tightly.

Suddenly, he is there, not more than eight steps away. My eyes are riveted to a tuft of hair six inches behind his shoulder, and I am only vaguely aware of the strain on my bad shoulder as the turkey feathers caress my cheek for an instant.

Someday, when the lion lays down with the lamb, when there are no wars or rumors of wars, this will not be necessary. But for now, in this world, it is necessary. The razor sharp two-blade broadhead makes a sickening "sssick!" sound as it slices deep on its path through the elk.

I slowly sink to the earth, ears straining for that horrifyingly wonderful sound. Seconds later it comes — a loud coarse cough. Then another and another, followed by the deafening death crash. I close my eyes and thank God for the quick death of a friend.

Chapter 15

The Legend of Wapiti-Tete
(A Work of Fiction)

Long before the smoke poles appeared that boomed like thunder and made magic to kill the elk, there was a tribe of Native Americans who lived a day's ride west of that crazy place where boiling waters flew up from the ground and smoke rose where there was no fire.

They were called the Elk Tribe, and their men were known among the other tribes for their great hunting ability. Animal skins and fresh meat usually hung from drying poles in their village. But even among this tribe of good hunters, one brave stood out from the others.

He was called, Wapiti, meaning elk. At his birth, the medicine man had looked down and exclaimed, "He will always be close to the Wapiti, so he shall be called one."

From his earliest days, Wapiti spent most of his free time exploring the land and its animals. He especially liked to study the vast elk herds that roamed the high country meadows. He killed his first elk at the age of 12 — a great feat for such a young man, and his reputation grew as his accomplishments in both war and hunting spread throughout neighboring tribes.

When winter snows made hunting difficult and other tribes starved, the Elk Tribe always had enough meat to eat, even when the elk were scarce. In those dreary days, Wapiti would wrap an elk hide around his shoulders, grab his bow, and trudge off into the winter wasteland for days. More than once, he was gone more than seven days, and the people thought for sure wolves or hunger had ended his

life. But each time, a weary Wapiti would come trudging into camp burdened with fresh elk meat for the tribe.

However, there was one bull, which many of the tribe felt had an evil spirit, that even Wapiti was not allowed to hunt. This old bull lived in a small basin tucked into a mountain pass. Several braves in the past had gone into that basin after the devil bull, but none had come out alive. It was rumored that one brave got close enough to put an arrow into the devil bull's shoulder before the enraged animal killed the hunter. Though that basin was covered with tasty camas plants, the women had to stay far away, or else the bull would charge out and kill them.

Though Wapiti had approached the elders several times for permission to hunt the devil bull, they had decided that he was too valuable as a warrior and hunter to risk getting killed. Besides, the elders had joked, that old bull was probably too tough to eat. Wapiti shrugged and bid his time. The elders seemed less and less opposed to his hunting the devil bull as his great feats of courage and hunting prowess piled up. Soon, they would give him permission to hunt the devil bull.

But it is the way among men, even among the Indians, that these feats were not appreciated by all. While the elders of the tribe and the women and children boasted of Wapiti's feats, there were a few braves whose toes curled with jealousy.

One of these braves was called Sinka, meaning lion. Sinka's heart burned with hate for Wapiti. Though Sinka was an excellent hunter and warrior, he could not quite measure up to Wapiti. So while other braves bragged up their brother, Sinka and his group secretly spoke evil of him.

Sinka rarely spoke to Wapiti. The other people knew this, and it caused the one blemish in the otherwise harmonious life of the Elk Tribe. Their rivalry had started early as boys growing up. Sinka had always been the bigger and stronger of his age group, and he had been brutal in his treatment of the other children, including Wapiti.

But as they approached the age of manhood, Wapiti began growing stronger and competed well against Sinka in all but the bow and arrow. Wapiti was by far the best bow and arrow shot, not only among the boys, but also among the mature braves. Visiting tribes would sit in wonder and watch Wapiti shoot his sinew and buffalo rib bow with uncanny accuracy. Everyone howled their approval as Wapiti hit the target again and again, but not Sinka.

He became convinced that it must be the fancy bow that made him such a good shot, so one night he crept into Wapiti's tepee and stole it. He buried it deep under the heavy mud along the river bank. But within days, Wapiti had built another bow, not as polished as the other had been, but it still sent each arrow to its mark with unerring accuracy.

Finally, Wapiti had returned one day dragging the carcass of a young bull elk behind his horse. This was a great feat for such a young man, and he was honored by the elders. That was too much for Sinka. His dislike for Wapiti that day turned to a jealous hate. The next afternoon while the younger boys were attending the horse herd, Sinka's hate boiled over and he picked a fight with Wapiti.

Sinka's first blows caught Wapiti by surprise, and he sat in the dust stunned by the suddenness of Sinka's blows. Blood flowed from his nose and mouth as he stared in confusion at the other boys. They stood stiff and quiet. No matter what their personal feelings might be, this was a fight for dominance among the new order of upcoming braves. Usually, each group agreed peacefully who their future leader would be. But not this time.

With great sadness and resignation, Wapiti regained his feet and faced an enraged Sinka. In the early going, Sinka's anger, and the damage done by his early blows, had tipped the fight in his favor. So it was with increasing fear that as the battle waged, Sinka began tasting blood in his own mouth. Eventually, Sinka lay in a heap at Wapiti's feet. It had been just a boyhood tussle, but from that day long ago to the present, neither man spoke to each other unless absolutely necessary.

Still, Sinka was greatly admired by many of the elders in the tribe, even though his hunting and fighting feats could not quite match Wapiti's. The day was approaching when the tribal elders would have to choose which man would be the new chief. But then love intervened.

It came in the form of a tall girl named Aria, who came to live with the tribe after her parents had died in a buffalo stampede. Aria was the most beautiful girl anyone had ever seen. Her skin was a golden coppery color, and her high cheekbones gave her an appearance of amusement. Unlike the other women who wore their long hair loose, Aria always wore her hair in a tight braid, which only made her look more exotic and beautiful to the young braves.

Aria immediately knew who she wanted for her husband. He was the one called Elk, who walked with such quiet dignity that people always glanced his way as he walked by. Children ran after him and grabbed at his hands, and older women smiled and handed him small pieces of jerky as he passed by. Older men nodded appreciably at him in honor of his accomplishments. In Aria's eyes, this brave named Wapiti was everything she could ever want in a husband.

Wapiti had also noticed her. He sent relatives to make sure she had heavy robes for the chilly nights, and when several younger braves began teasing her, it took but one glowering stare from Wapiti to stop them. During the nightly powwows, they stared longingly at each other across the huge fire, forbidden by tribal law to court each other until the elders gave their approval.

But it wasn't as simple as that. The family of Sinka had already approached the elders for permission to join Sinka and Aria in marriage. One night at the council fire, they brought great riches as a dowry, and the elders were truly impressed. Finally, a meeting was held, and it was publicly announced that Sinka had sought Aria for a wife. If anyone else wanted to be considered, he should step forward. No one immediately came forward, and Aria's heart sank. The elders were ready to pass judgement on the marriage when Wapiti stepped forward and said, "I would have this girl for my wife."

Sinka was angered, not only by Wapiti's intrusion, but also by the sudden glowing look Aria had given him. Sinka countered, "I asked first. Your family is poor. You have no dowry except for a few sickly ponies. You have nothing to offer."

Wapiti knew Sinka was correct. Something of great value had to be given when a bride was requested. Wapiti's mind raced for an answer, and then he stood tall and replied, "I will go out after the devil elk and count coup."

There was a loud gasp from among the people, and many began to protest. "It would be suicide!" "No one can get close to that bull. He is bad medicine, sent by our enemies to torment us!"

A cunning smile came over Sinka's face. He stepped forward and said, "If you can count coup on that bull, you will have favor over me, and my dowry shall pass over to you."

Even at that very uncharacteristic offer from Sinka, Wapiti's friends showed no great appreciation because other braves had tried to hunt the devil bull — and not returned.

Wapiti put out his hand, palm up, and poured a bright reddish powder onto his palm. He said, "And this shall be proof that I counted coup on the devil bull. The bull will be seen with my ochra hand print on his rump. And then after all the people have seen the hand print, I will kill this devil elk to make our passage safe through the divide once more." A rousing cheer arose, and the people surged forward to touch the man who would do the impossible and touch an elk, especially that one.

But not Sinka. He slipped away to meet with a few of his friends. That night, there was a great feast and celebration. A few of the braves who were Wapiti's friends watched Sinka closely because they remembered long ago how he had sneaked into the tepee that night to steal Wapiti's bow. Sinka feasted and danced, and as Wapiti watched his rival, he thought that maybe the feud had finally ended. At that exact moment, a dark form slipped under the buffalo hide covering Wapiti's tepee. A razor sharp knife glistened in the moonlight, and its owner carefully rubbed the string of Wapiti's bow. The knife easily sliced halfway through the sinew bowstring.

The camp was astir at dawn the next morning, to watch Wapiti jump upon his pony. He gave one long glance back at Aria and then dug his heels into the horse's flanks. A great cheer arose and the people surged forward behind Wapiti.

Hundreds of people quietly rimmed the rocks above the small basin where the devil elk lived. They trembled as his bellowing bugles echoed off the sheer rock mountain rising above them. They trembled even more when they saw the form of Wapiti easing down through the rocks.

The devil bull was not difficult to find. Wapiti could feel the earth shake long before he entered the bull's lair. He circled to the downwind side and eased forward. A huge harem of cows milled through the dense forest between Wapiti and the devil bull. Suddenly, a cow spotted him and barked a warning. The huge bull whirled and came trotting forward to rout the intruder, be it man or bear.

The massive animal stopped and bellowed out a warning. His mighty head swung back and forth, searching for his next victim. Wapiti dared a peek and gasped. The bull was almost twice as large as the other bulls he'd killed. On the bull's right shoulder was a large bulge where cartilage covered the old arrow wound.

Wapiti strung his bow and drew his favorite arrow from his quiver. He carefully surveyed the terrain ahead and decided the bull would come forward through a narrow opening between two brush thickets. He eased backward into a small clump of three trees. His foot struck something and he stumbled. He glanced down and gasped. A skull grinned back at him, and he noticed rotting rawhide and beads on the ground where he stood.

He knew it was bad medicine to be standing on top of that murdered brave, but he had no choice because the devil bull had heard him slip and was looking suspiciously in his direction. With trembling hand he cupped his mouth and turned away. The devil bull was first startled, then enraged, when a shrill bugle floated back to him through the crisp mountain air. A deep, guttural growl rumbled up from deep in his throat. He lowered his head and viciously rammed a nearby pine tree. His eight point rack bent and then broke the four-inch-thick tree.

Again the young bull bugled from just out of sight. The devil bull bellowed a response and stomped forward. He entered a small opening between two brush thickets, and had just passed three pine trees, when he felt the hard slap on his rump. As quick as a cat, he whirled and rammed the clump of trees. Though momentarily stunned by the force of the blow, Wapiti scooted left and carefully drew his bow. It was the same bow he'd used to kill many huge bull elk. It was extra powerful and its medicine had always been good. Wapiti slowly drew back on the bowstring, and was almost to full draw, when the bow suddenly exploded. The arrow and bow fell harmlessly to the ground. One quick glance as the neat cut marks on the sinew string alerted Wapiti to the treachery that had been done last night.

An instant later the devil bull was after him. He barely had time to dive behind the three trees before the massive antlers rammed into them, causing bark and wood splinters to fly. Again and again the bull pummeled the trees. Wapiti knew what must be done. He drew out his knife and when the bull rammed the trees again, he struck the side of the elk's neck. The blade went in deep, but the bull instinctively jerked back, pulling the knife and Wapiti with him.

Wapiti quickly regained his feet, but the knife stayed embedded in the devil bull's neck. He dove for the trees, but the bull's three-foot long royal dagger point rammed deep into his side. Pinned to the ground, he struggled to reach the knife in the bull's neck. The bull eased back a few steps, as if to retreat, then viciously rammed his antlers into the hapless fallen brave. Wapiti screamed in agony, and far above on the rim rocks, the people cheered because they thought they'd heard a victory cry.

Eventually, the cries from the small basin died down and the people peered down, hoping to see their hero emerge. They gasped when the devil bull stomped into the open. Suddenly, a brave cried, "There! On his rump! A hand print!" A great cry of joy arose among the people, but it slowly subsided into a murmur of worry because Wapiti had promised that he would kill the bull as soon as the people had seen that he had counted coup.

The devil bull took a step forward, then stumbled. He regained his feet and looked up at the people. He extended his huge head to bellow a bugle of defiance, but the angry bugle died in his throat and he pitched forward. He lay on his side, and it was then that the people saw the knife embedded in his neck. They feared that something had gone dreadfully wrong.

Eventually, Wapiti's friends entered the thicket and found the fallen hero. Not a bone in his body had gone unbroken, so vicious had been the devil bull's revenge. The knife had barely nicked the bull's jugular vein, and it took a long time for the wound to drain the life from the elk. Too long.

It was then that the braves found the bow with the partially severed bowstring, and a great howl of outrage arose among them. The braves showed the partially cut bowstring to the elders. Without speaking a word or looking directly at him, they ordered Sinka's belongings to be dumped in a heap beyond the ring of tepees — a sign that he was not welcome among the people of the Elk tribe any more. Insolently, Sinka and his cohorts strode past the people, shouting threats and making obscene gestures as they galloped away.

Aria refused to leave the place where Wapiti had died. Her

high pitched shrieks and moaning wails echoed through the narrow rock canyons for many days and nights. When a party was sent to bring her back, they found no sign of her. But when the wind blew through the narrow pass in the divide, the people swore they could hear her shrieking moans.

The elders met in counsel to decide some way to honor their beloved, fallen Wapiti. Finally, they chose to honor him unlike anyone else in the history of their tribe. They changed his name to Wapiti-Tete, which means "Touches Elk." For many generations, young children sat in speechless awe as an elder told the story of the greatest elk hunter who ever lived.

The arrow-filled bones of Sinka and his group were found the next spring, and it was generally believed that a raiding war party must have surprised them, but there were a few of Wapiti's friends who always grew silent and left the tepee whenever the conversation turned to the demise of Sinka.

Years later, when the white men came, they asked about the strange moaning shrieks that echoed off the rock walls high above the pass in the divide. The Indians told them the story of Wapiti-Tete and Aria. Misinterpreting their words, the white men thought her name was Mariah, and hence, the shrieking, moaning of the wind in the lonely high country is called MARIAH!

And even to this day, there are reports of modern bowhunters encountering bull elk with a curious birthmark on their rumps. It is reddish, and it almost looks like the hand print of a man.

The elk was misnamed by early European explorers, who thought it resembled the European moose, which was called "ELK."

Chapter 16

Fascinating Elk Facts

Much of the joy of elk hunting comes from being intimately acquainted with this fascinating species we call the elk. Much of the information may seem trivial, having little to do with making the reader a better hunter, but as we read more about the elk, we gain a deeper love and appreciation for this giant deer.

Origin of the Name ELK

Biologically speaking, it was pure butchery to call this animal an elk. The confusion began as early as the first European settlers to North America. They immediately identified it as a near cousin of the European red deer. The problem arose when some early explorers and settlers began to call this large deer an "elk." In most European languages, elk referred to the European moose. Subsequent discovery of the North American moose only compounded the problem.

For quite some time, naturalists called it everything from a "Hind" to a "Moose" to an "Elk." The debate disappeared after the Lewis & Clark expedition returned. Their diaries referred to the big deer as an elk, and the term stuck. So, like many English language terms, an elk is really not an elk.

Many naturalists in the 1800's tried to differentiate between the European elk and the misnamed American elk by adopting the Shawnee Indian name "Wapiti" for the American elk, which translated means "white rump." Many elk lovers have chosen to call it by its Indian name, Wapiti, but for the most part, the term ELK is the accepted norm.

Historic Distribution

Various subspecies of the American elk inhabited virtually the entire North American Continent from Mexico to Alaska. Only in the most swampy areas, such as Florida and southern Louisiana, has no archeological evidence of elk been found.

The Eastern elk was found in all the states east of and including Wisconsin, Iowa, Missouri, Arkansas and Louisiana. This species was exterminated by the late 1800's by settlers and hunters.

The Manitoban elk, averaging about 800 pounds, was once found throughout the midwestern states of the Dakotas, Nebraska, Kansas, Oklahoma, and Texas; through the eastern half of Montana, Wyoming and Colorado and north into Canada.

The Manitoban elk had smaller antlers than today's Rocky Mountain elk, though its size was larger. Uncontrolled hunting sent this subspecies into virtual extinction by 1900, though some scientists believe there is some evidence that they may have bred with the Rocky Mountain elk.

The Merriam elk inhabited the arid land of Arizona, New Mexico, Texas and Mexico. Uncontrolled hunting and cattle grazing

The Rocky Mountain elk inhabits the mountainous West.

sent the Merriam elk into extinction by 1906. Those areas where Merriam elk once lived are now home to the transplanted Rocky Mountain elk.

The Tule elk inhabited the coastal marshes of California. A mature Tule bull elk weighs only about 550 pounds. Its antlers are much smaller and more scraggly looking than the Rocky Mountain elk. By 1875, this species was on the verge of extinction, but a local rancher took an interest in the Tule elk and protected the few remaining animals on his property.

Today, there is a small, but growing herd of Tule elk in California, and very limited hunting is now allowed to eliminate surplus animals because local ranchers and farmers are generally intolerant of encroachment on their croplands by the Tule elk.

The Rocky Mountain elk inhabited the mountainous regions of the western states. The rugged terrain where they called home saved this species from extinction by market hunters, and these elk were the seed crop that biologists used to reintroduce the elk back into many of its former haunts.

The Roosevelt elk inhabited the dense coastal rain forests of Washington, Oregon, California, and the Canadian coast. This is the largest of the elk, at about 1,100 pounds. The dense forests protected the Roosevelt elk from the onslaught of market hunters, and this species now is thriving in much of its historical habitat.

Near Extermination

Elimination of its native habitat and uncontrolled hunting exterminated most of the elk from the eastern half of America before most western expansion began. However, pioneers moving over the endless prairie were astounded by the vast herds of buffalo and elk that roamed the grasslands of the West.

With this western migration came one of the most shameful and tragic eras of wildlife exploitation. Hide hunters slaughtered hundreds of thousands of buffalo for nothing more than their hides. It was estimated that 99% of the meat from slaughtered buffalo was wasted. As the buffalo harvest dwindled, market hunters turned their attention to elk. Eastern tanners found the elk hide to be much more pliable than buffalo, so they began paying $7.00 for an elk hide, as opposed to only $4.00 for a buffalo hide.

The ideal elk herd contains 40% immature bulls, 40% mature bulls, and 20% older mature herd bulls.

Elk by the thousands were slaughtered. The only edible part that was saved was the tongue. By 1890, elk were thought by many to be extinct. It was only in those remote pockets of the Rocky Mountain wilderness that a few small herds of elk still lived. Fortunately, they were not pursued, and today, their descendants comprise most of the western elk herd, which now numbers about a million.

Early Elk Hunters

Native American hunters valued and pursued the elk long before the first white men ever set foot on North American soil. Archeological sites throughout America have uncovered many elk artifacts ranging from tools to ornaments. However, the elk did not figure into the Indian lifestyle as much as deer or buffalo because the elk was too difficult to hunt on foot.

That all changed with the coming of the horse. The Indians now had a method of transportation to follow the constantly roaming elk and hunt it at times when it was most vulnerable. Strangely, the advent of the horse-mounted Indian also created a large increase in elk numbers due to the Indians penchant for using fire to create grasslands to feed their horses.

Once the enemy of the Indian on foot, fire now became a tool to clear forested tracts of land where grass grew back because the horse-mounted Indian was able to outrun the windswept fires. This not only suited the needs of the horse, but it also suited the grass-loving elk. In areas where only a few elk had roamed, now large herds roamed the land.

However, even on horseback, the Indian did not have easy hunting for the wily elk. Unlike the buffalo, which could be confused and stampeded en masse and then shot by horse-mounted braves, the elk tended to scatter and head for the thickets or mountains where horse pursuit was hazardous. In fact many tribes, such as the Chippewa and Sarsi, considered it dangerous and inefficient to hunt the elk on horseback.

Other tribes, such as the Blackfeet, Comanche, Crow and Sioux adapted their horse hunting techniques to suit plains elk hunting. Rather than charging an elk herd, these Indians often broke up into small units and circled the herd. One small group of Indians then rode into the open and flushed the elk, which usually ran for cover. In that cover, braves were hidden along strategic game trails to ambush passing elk. Other horse-mounted riders cut off the fleeing elk and shot them with arrows as they passed by.

The Indian bow and arrow was best suited for short range, often point-blank, shooting at buffalo or deer. It was often ineffective when shot at the larger elk at ranges beyond 20 yards. Lewis & Clark mentioned this fact in their diaries, and noted that several of the elk their men had shot carried old arrow wounds that had healed over.

While it may be romantic to think of the American Indian charging in close pursuit across the prairie after a bull elk, the fact remains that more elk were harvested in jumps, snares, and traps. At many jump sites, evidence was clear that elk were often herded en masse off cliffs. Indians also liked to chase elk into box canyons where brush corrals and hidden archers awaited them. Another exciting method of hunting elk was snaring. An Indian would climb

Four year old cows have proven to be the best mothers, biologically and protection-wise.

a tree over a game trail, and when the elk were chased that way, he would drop a rawhide noose down and snare an elk as it ran by.

Though much has been written about the Indians' wars with the white man, it should be understood that the loss of the Indian's food source, mainly buffalo and elk, was a leading cause of the Indian's demise. Hide hunters who slaughtered herds of elk and buffalo left the plains a vast wasteland for returning war parties, and it was not long before the once proud Native Americans were begging the U.S. Government for food.

Herd Dynamics

The object of wildlife biologists is to maintain an elk herd at optimum levels in relation to hunting pressure and environment. Obviously, this concept is easier to write down than it is to accomplish. State game commissions, and their subsequent management practices, are often used as political footballs. More often than not, the management of the elk herd is tipped in favor of the human hunter than the establishment of a healthy elk herd.

Biologists describe a healthy elk herd as a group of elk

consisting of about one hundred bulls per two hundred cows. Only in those regulated hunting units, mostly in the Southwest, is that average a reality. Within that male group, there should be about 40% immature bulls in the one to four year old range. About 40% of the bulls should then be in the early prime age group from five to seven years old. This group of bulls is fully mature, but not yet ready to compete for the leadership of the herd. About 20% of the bulls fall into the "herd bull" category. These are seven to ten year old animals whose antler growth has reached its maximum.

In most areas of the country, it is rare to find one bull that might be six years old in that number of elk, let alone 40%. This is due to the practice of managing the elk herd more for massive sport hunting than optimum biological balance of the herd. It may sound impressive for a state like Colorado to boast a harvest of 50,000 elk annually from a herd of 200,000 animals, but such massive harvesting keeps the bull hierarchy from maturing.

Reproduction

Reproduction is the process that insures the future of the elk herd, but its dynamics is often so fragile as to be frightening. So many intangible factors play into the success, or failure, of each year's calf crop.

One thing we know for sure, the best seed is passed on by the mature, older bulls. Ask any farmer about that. However, it is also a biological fact that a spike bull is fully capable of delivering his puny sperm into a cow elk if the mature bulls are eliminated from the herd.

The dynamics of reproduction occur among the cows. A yearling cow is fully capable of mating. However, many complications occur for these first-time mothers, and it is not unusual for yearling cows to lose their calves due to a host of factors ranging from lack of protection from predators to nutritional deficiencies. Four year old cows have proven to be the best mothers. They are in their prime of life, and they've been around long enough to kick the brains out of a marauding coyote.

Though it is hard for humans to accept it, most calf crops will experience upwards to a 50% mortality rate. That's one reason why hunters who see cows without calves often misinterpret this to mean that the bulls are being harassed too much by bowhunters to have time enough to mate the cows.

Intense calf mortality studies have found that poor weather and poor nutrition usually take their toll on calves during those first critical weeks of life. Also, predators play a large part in calf mortality in springtime.

Last June, I spent two weeks in Yellowstone park videoing grizzly bears as they roamed the elk calving grounds hunting newborn. That, folks, was tough for this elk-loving hunter to watch as a particular grizzly would run down and kill one or two helpless calves each day for two weeks until the little fellows grew strong enough to outrun the bull-like rush of the grizzly.

One study in Central Idaho discovered that upwards to 40% of the spring calf crop was being killed by black bears. When that hunting unit allowed two bear kills per hunter, the calf crop improved.

Antler Growth

An elk's antlers begin to grow immediately after his old antlers are shed in late spring. Once the antlers fall, a bloody, pulpy wound surrounded by bone, called the pedicle, becomes visible. Within days, a velvet covering protects the pedicle and this covering can be seen raising with each passing day.

A very complex process of nutrition takes place in the bull's body to accommodate antler growth at this time. The entire antler growing process is triggered by a small amount of testosterone, produced by the testicles, which reaches the tissue inside the pedicle and induces growth. Various other chemical compounds, far too complex for the average person to understand, contribute to the intricate growing process.

The antlers at this early stage are covered with a soft velvet membrane. Both the antlers and pedicle grow at this time as a result of cartilage tissue being deposited by a network of blood vessels. In fact, in the velvet stage, an elk's antlers are pliable and warm to the touch.

As the bull's antlers reach maximum growth, an increase in testosterone levels actually cuts off the blood flow to the antlers, and they die, leaving behind dead bone. When the bull rubs the velvet off the hard antler, its color is ivory white. The antler is colored by the reaction of oxygen with juices from plants and trees rubbed during the shedding process. As soon as the bull rubs the velvet off his antlers, he is capable of mating because the testosterone that had been delivered to the antlers, now courses it way through the bull's body. The bull needs only a cow in heat from this time on to complete the mating process.

Elk Physiology

Elk are extremely flexible ruminants (vegetation eaters). They fare well in a variety of environments from the hardwoods of Pennsylvania, to the western Rockies, to the desert country of the Southwest. This is possible because elk belong to the ungulate family of mixed feeders. They are capable of feeding on both browse and grass, though they prefer grass.

As such, the elk is extraordinarily adaptable to a variety of terrain because its stomach will accept and process both grass and woody pulp at the same time and turn this matter into nutrition. I have discovered, much to my delight and relief, that the feeding and

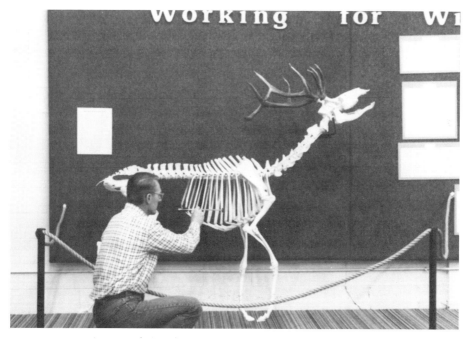

An elk's skeleton is narrow and long, which suits the elk well for fast running.

Even though elk may always look healthy and strong, they are not free from diseases and parasites.

bedding urges of elk are virtually identical for high country Northern Rockies elk and flatland desert elk of New Mexico.

Generally, elk have about four major feeding stages spread out through 24 hours. It is a mistake to think that elk get out of their beds in evening to feed, eat through the night, and early morning, and then bed down for the day. The greatest period of activity may be during the late and early daylight hours, but that is only because the elk are moving from their bed to feeding areas, eating as they go. Because an elk's stomach is relatively small, it will have to refill at least four times each day.

The conservation success of elk during the past years is due not only to man's efforts, but also to the amazing adaptability of the elk to successfully feed on just about any plant or grass in front of its nose.

Skeleton

The skeletal configuration of the elk is elongated and narrow, which suits the elk well for fast running over the prairie. A mature bull elk's skeleton will weigh over 100 pounds. Native Americans use virtually every part of the elk's skeleton for everything from hoes, to awls, to clubs.

Dentition

Elk dentition is normal for the Cervus family of plant and grass eaters, with sharp flat front teeth for snipping off vegetation, and hard rounded molars for grinding it into pulp. One of the most curious aspects of elk dentition are the two rounded canine teeth found in the upper jaw of both the cow and bull. Scientists are not quite sure of the purpose of these canines, or whistler, teeth. It is very unusual for an animal to have both antlers and canine teeth. These canine teeth are ivory and valued for use as jewelry.

Eventually, an elk's teeth wear down, and this fact, more than any other, limits the life expectancy of an adult. Eight year old bulls have been killed which were in poor physical condition in places where nutritious feed abounded. Upon closer examination, it was discovered that their teeth were worn down below the gums, making it very difficult and painful to feed.

Diseases & Parasites

To the casual observer elk look like they're always in good health, but it is unreasonable to think that the Wapiti would be able to escape the ravages of disease and parasites. Elk are susceptible to sickness and death from a variety of disorders.

Specifically, elk are susceptible to the deadly anthrax and brucellosis diseases. Anthrax occurs naturally in ground spores and when ingested by an elk, causes quick death. Brucellosis is a far more common and serious disease and currently infects many of our major elk herds. The wintering Jackson Hole elk herd was found to have a 50% infection rate, while tests have shown that many elk in and around Yellowstone National Park carry the brucellosis virus.

Brucellosis is a much feared disease among ranchers because it causes sterilization and abortions among female stock. While many diseases are not, in reality, as dangerous as they sound, the brucellosis bacteria is for real.

There is a serious political flap currently being waged in Yellowstone concerning brucellosis infected bison and elk. Area ranchers fear that these wild animals, which often leave the Park in winter when feed becomes scarce, will spread the brucellosis bacteria to domestic cattle. Today, migrating bison are being shot when they move onto private land. Animal rights extremists howl in outrage over these killings, but until a better method comes along, this is the only way to keep domestic cattle free from contracting the brucellosis bacteria.

Several parasites latch onto elk and use them as hosts. Arthropods from ticks to mites are fairly common among elk. However, only the mite has the potential to cause harm to the elk herd. Massive infestations of the microscopic mites cause scabies, or mange, and pose a real danger to infected elk herds.

In addition, roundworms, lungworms and arterial worms can also cause death among elk. In these situations, the primary transmitter is the bloodthirsty horsefly. In areas where horseflys are not numerous, incidents of these parasitic infections are low.

Recreational Potential

The recreational potential of elk is great throughout North America, even besides the obvious practice of sport hunting for elk.

The recreation potential for elk is great, even beside the obvious sport of elk hunting.

Many parks feature elk as a viewing attraction for tourists. Just about every visitor to Yellowstone National Park asks where the elk can be found. The sleek, robust physique and large size, plus their herding tendency, make the Wapiti a favorite of everyone.

In several national parks in the West, the month of September is a magical time of year when the bull elk rut, and the golden frost-burned hills echo with the bugling challenge of rutting bulls. Many visitors actually hold off and take their vacations in the fall in order to view this awesome spectacle.

As more elk transplants occur in eastern states, the viewing potential for tourists has increased dramatically. Even small Mom & Pop country stores are getting into the elk viewing business. I know of several small stores whose owners have a few penned elk next door. It's amazing how many travelers stop by these places to view the elk — and purchase goodies.

It is difficult to put a dollar value on the recreational potential of the elk. We know that many hundreds of millions of dollars are spent by sport hunters in pursuit of elk every year. However, much of the reason for family vacations to western national parks is to view

One day, the hunter may have to compete with the wolf in the field, and in the courts, for the right to hunt elk.

the mighty bull elk in a natural setting.

Elk Population Dynamics

Elk are extremely prolific, and since they are big animals with big appetites, the potential to overpopulate and overgraze habitat is great. So far, sport hunting has been used as the primary tool to keep elk numbers compatible with habitat.

Of course, there will always be a few slight imbalances, where maybe too many elk are left, or too few, after hunting season. But generally, state wildlife agencies have done a good job of providing hunters with enough elk to hunt, and the elk with enough habitat to exist.

The animal rights, anti-hunting faction has made many inroads against sportsmen. As a trapper, I watched in frustration and bewilderment, as my beloved sport was trod down, maligned, and eliminated in several states. And all the while hunters turned a deaf ear to the pleas of the outnumbered trappers.

Now, the monster has come to roost right in the laps of sport hunters. Lion and bear seasons have been voted out of existence in some states, while other states' deer seasons are being challenged in court. Up to this point, the animal rights faction usually ran into a brick wall when wildlife biologists explained to a judge that big game numbers had to be controlled to avoid crop and habitat damage. Hunting was the preferred method of population control because it needed very little in-field work by professionals. In other words, the hunters quickly entered an area, eliminated the overpopulation of animals, and quickly left the area in its natural state.

As I have mentioned, the federally mandated reintroduction of the gray wolf may have far-reaching consequences on elk hunting as a herd management tool. As wolf numbers increase, these voracious predators may rival sport hunters for the surplus animals in a given area. And if it should ever come to a judicial decision, the welfare of the wolf will probably take precedence over sport hunting.

Appendix A

Recommended Elk Outfitters

Author's Note: This list of recommended outfitters is relatively short, for a good reason. These are outfits that I have either worked with personally, or someone I know and trust has worked with them.

For example, East Fork Outfitters is the outfit I worked with last fall when I killed a dandy bull for the video "Elk Hunting With The Experts." I can personally vouch for this outfit as being top notch, with good guides and plenty of rutting elk to hunt.

On the other hand, I have not yet worked with Eagle Spirit Outfitters of Colorado. However, my good friend, John Sloan, was there last year and killed a nice bull. He spoke highly of all aspects of this outfit. Consequently, I have listed them because a personal friend told me, "Yes, they are legitimate."

This is not to say that these are the only good outfitters. There are others out there. I just don't know who they are. However, I hear horror stories over the phone every year from elk hunters who hired the outfitter from hell! Seven days in a miserable camp, no bulls seen or heard, disrespectful guides — and they still had to pay $2,000!

That's why I included this list. If you plan to use an outfitter, these outfits have proven themselves — at least to me.

ARIZONA
Penrod Outfitting
David Penrod
P.O. Box 1014
Pinetop, AZ 85935
602-367-3220

U.S. Outfitters
George Taulman
Box 4204
Taos, NM87571
1-800-845-9929

COLORADO
Eagle Spirit Outfitters
Miles & Susie Hogan
P.O Box 775792
Steamboat Springs, CO 80477
970-870-8241

Proline Excursions
Paul Howard
P.O. Box 5323
Wheat Ridge, CO 80034
303-423-8322

Mountain West Outfitting
10433 W. Arkansas Drive
Lakewood, CO 80232
303-988-2874

Slater Creek Cattle Co.
P.O. Box 1407
Craig, CO 81626
970-824-3536

U.S. Outfitters
George Taulman
Box 4204
Taos, NM 87571
1-800-845-9929

IDAHO
Bear Creek Outfitters
Lyle Phelps
4105 Three Mile Rd.
Wieppe, ID 83533
208-435-4610

MONTANA
Bull Mountain Outfitters
Mike Murphy
Box 286
Mussellshell, MT 59059
406-947-3337

East Fork Outfitters
Mark McKee
P.O. Box 33
Sula, MT 59871
1-800-763-3688

Lazy T4 Outfitters
Spence Trogdon
Box 116
Victor, MT 59875
406-642-3586

Montana Experience Excursions
Carl Mann
234 Ridgeway
Lolo, MT 59847
406-273-6966

Jack Atcheson & Sons
International Hunting Consultants
3210 Ottawa Street
Butte, MT 59701
406-782-3498

NEW MEXICO
C.S. Cattle Company
Randy Davis
Rt. 1, Box 55
Cimarron, NM 87714
505-376-2595

U.S. Outfitters
George Taulman
Box 4204
Taos, NM 87571
1-800-845-9929

UTAH
Wasatch Outfitters
Fred John
3336 Grammercy Ave.
Ogden, Utah 84403
801-394-4262

WYOMING
Bliss Creek Outfitters
Ken Doud
326 Diamond Basin Rd.
Cody, WY 82414
307-527-6103

Appendix B

Recommended Books, Videos, Equipment

Below is a list of recommended books, videos and elk hunting equipment to better prepare the prospective elk hunter for his upcoming western hunt. In addition to the manufacturers' addresses listed, many of these items are available in many archery shops, sporting goods stores, or from mail order catalogs.

Books
1. Western Hunting Guide, by Mike Lapinski
2. Radical Elk Hunting Strategies, by Mike Lapinski
3. Successful Big Game Hunting, by Duncan Gilchrist
4. Montana Hunting Guide, by Dale Burk
5. Bugling For Elk, by Dwight Schuh
6. Field Care Handbook, by Bill Sager and Duncan Gilchrist
7. Elk Hunting in The Northern Rockies, by Ed Wolff

These books can be ordered from Stoneydale Press, 523 Main Street, Box 188, Stevensville, MT 59870 (1-800-735-7006)

Videos
1. Rocky Mountain Elk, Their Life Story
2. Elk Hunting In The Rocky Mountains
3. Early Season Elk Hunting
4. Radical Elk Hunting Strategies Video
5. Point-Blank Elk
6. Archery Elk, The Dream Hunt
7. Elk Hunting With The Experts (New release in 1996)

These videos can be ordered from Stoneydale Press, 523 Main Street, Box 188, Stevensville, MT 59870 (1-800-735-7006)